HITLER AVATĀRA

Martin Friedrich

HITLER AVATĀRA

Martin Friedrich

Clemens & Blair, LLC

— 2023 —

CLEMENS & BLAIR, LLC

Clemens & Blair, LLC, is a non-profit educational publisher.
www.clemensandblair.com

Library of Congress Cataloging-in-Publication Data

Friedrich, Martin
Hitler Avatāra

p. cm.
Includes bibliographical references

ISBN 979-8987-7263-41
(pbk.: alk. paper)

Printing number: 9 8 7 6 5 4 3 2 1

Printed in the United States of America on acid-free paper.

Dedicated to Adolf Hitler — the greatest of all of us,
because he was not one of us.

This is our preparation before becoming the lawgivers of the future and the lords of the earth; if not we, at least our children.
— Friedrich Nietzsche, *The Will to Power*

For this faith in the victory of the beautiful I will struggle for dear life, and nothing in the world will wrench it from me.
— Søren Kierkegaard, *Either/Or, Part II*

[Adolf Hitler was] a Warrior for Mankind and a Preacher of the Gospel of Justice to all Nations.... We, his close followers, bow our heads before his memory.
— Knut Hamsun, *Aftenposten*, 1945

CONTENTS

FOREWORD

THOMAS DALTON

For many people, past and present, Adolf Hitler was an exceptional human being: a leader, a guide, a visionary, a prophet, a genius, perhaps a figure of spiritual significance, perhaps even a kind of secular divinity. There have been a number of such people in the past; one thinks of the Pharaoh Akhenaten, Plato, Michelangelo, Mozart, Nietzsche — men whose skills and abilities take one's breath away. Hitler, of course, was more controversial than such men, but he was also, arguably, more consequential. It would be hard to find a man that has had a greater impact on the history of civilization; perhaps Alexander the Great, perhaps Julius Caesar, perhaps Genghis Khan — but few others. And living so close to the present, we naturally feel Hitler's legacy more directly than those others of centuries past.

But what if Hitler was even more than this? We can let our speculations unfold: What if he was a truly divine being, someone godlike, perhaps a god himself? Jesus, of course, was said to be such a man, but we now understand him to be a Jewish construction at the hands of "Saint" Paul, built around a rather ordinary rabbi who got himself crucified. By contrast, Hitler was a real, flesh-and-blood man, but also someone, conceivably, with a truly divine spark at his core. Coming from a position of humility, no wealth, and no formal training, he rose to inconceivable heights of influence and power — something apparently impossible for an ordinary mortal. Clearly, the gods were with him.

Yes, of course, Hitler did fall in the end, brought down by the combined might of the world's industrial powers, driven to obscene levels of hatred by world Jewry. He tried to avert great suffering, and to raise up Europe's Germanic people to unprecedented heights of art, culture, and civility — but he was stopped by the global masters of hatred, vengeance, and debasement. Fortunately for us, though, his words and his vision have survived. Hitler lost the battle, but the larger war goes on. Hitler's legacy is still open;

the plan has yet to fully play itself out; no one yet knows how it will all end.

But now, in the present, we may speculate on 'Hitler as divine being,' 'Hitler as god,' 'Hitler as an avatar' — a divinity incarnate. And this is precisely what our author, Martin Friedrich, has done in this book. Testing the fine line between fact and fiction, between vision and reality, Friedrich explores what it might mean to see Hitler as an avatar, a divinity, a god-man come to Earth. For 2,000 years, much of Western civilization has been captivated and entranced by another god-man, Jesus — whom many took as absolute reality, and to whom many dedicated their lives. But that god-man was a true fiction, a Jewish concoction, intended to undermine and debase the Gentile morality of the day. Friedrich, by contrast, takes a very real and very great man, and asks: What would it mean if Hitler was a divine being, a holy spirit made tangible, a god in human form? If a fake avatar like Jesus can hold such power, imagine the potential of a real avatar, a real man with godlike powers.

'Avatar' is an interesting word with a long pedigree.[1] It derives from the Sanskrit word avatāra (which Friedrich prefers), meaning 'he that descends' or 'he who crosses over (into the material plane).' The word came to prominence in Hindu literature of the 500s AD, where it was most frequently applied to the god Vishnu — the deity known as 'the pervader' or 'the sustainer.' In Hindu mythology, Vishnu Avatāra appears on Earth in human form in times of crisis, in order to reestablish dharma (justice, righteousness) among humanity. Vishnu descends when the power of evil threatens to defeat that of the good; he then restores the cosmic balance, and departs once more to his heavenly realm.

In a similar fashion, Friedrich imagines that Hitler Avatāra likewise came to Earth to establish eternal justice among his people. Appearing among the beleaguered Germans, in just six short years — 1933 to 1939 — he singlehandedly raised them up to a world power, a true light unto the nations. This was possible only

---

[1] The word, sadly, has become trivialized in recent years, coming to represent science fiction characters, cartoonish figures, and even 'profile pictures' of computer users.

by defeating the Jewish hydra that had thoroughly suffocated the German nation, from at least the 1850s. Employing an apparently superhuman power, Hitler crushed the hydra, purified his people, and restored to them life, hope, and — *a future*. His rapid success was too much for global Jewry; they understood that a shining success in one nation would lead to similar actions in other nations, and that this would in turn mean utter defeat for Jews worldwide.

For Jewry, it was a life-or-death moment. Thus they had to conspire among nations to bring Hitler down. Once they did that, they then colluded to defame his image, to disparage his successes, to slander his greatness, to distort his truths, and to so confuse the masses that they might now, subconsciously, equate the great man — one of the greatest to walk the planet — with 'evil.' The Jews, with their cleverness and tenacity at portraying lies as truth, have so far managed to create a false historical narrative — complete with a fake 'Holocaust' — that has been swallowed unthinkingly by the masses of the West.

But this situation cannot endure. Lies cannot forever pass as truth. Greatness cannot long be slandered as evil. The time of the shifty, conniving, malicious liars is nearing an end. From on high, Vishnu surveys his realm; the time for justice is at hand.

Hitler the man is dead. But Hitler Avatāra lives on, inspiring the Germanic people — and indeed all noble Aryans — to rise up, stiffen their spine, shake off the millstone of global Jewry, and strive for greatness. All is in our hands; we need only act.

INTRODUCTION

As the Paradox He is an extremely unhistorical person. But this is the difference between poetry and reality: contemporaneousness.
— Søren Kierkegaard, *Training in Christianity*

The truth must suffer in every generation; and though it manifests myriad ways, truth remains unchanged: it is the presence of God. Truth suffers because of man's descent into godlessness; from age to age, man descends further, distancing himself ever more from God. As all of recorded history is a history of this darkest of ages, the Kali-Yuga, even man's greatest triumphs are marked with imperfection; the basest acts — which are more prevalent and, further, reflect the rule that quantity, through sheer numbers, outshines quality — dominate daily life. It is therefore necessary for God to appear on earth, as Avatāra, to defend the interests of his adherents and the quality that remains on earth, which reflect his timeless image; God's descent to man is periodic; God's presence among those who uphold his tenets is eternal. The difference between God and man is potency: How much truth is present? In this way, man is a vessel for God. But God chooses his form; he chooses when and where he appears; and his message is always tailored to the understanding of the people amongst whom he manifests.

Krishna, as Avatāra of God, assured Arjuna: "Whenever and wherever there is a decline in religious practice ... and a predominant rise of irreligion — at that time I descend Myself."[1] God appears of his own will to combat the devilry of the day; combat is necessary in God's creation because God wills it. Life is struggle; therefore, life is participation in the Divine. More precisely, combat is necessary because the Demiurge-Jehovah, who stands against

---

[1] Bhagavad Gita, IV.7, translated by A.C. Bhaktivedanta Swami Prabhupada (all Gita translations are his unless otherwise noted).

God and seeks to usurp creation, has dominion over our earthly outpost; in this way, earth is the provenance for the Cosmic Struggle wherein God realizes itself, the truth reveals itself, and man communes with God. The Vedas, revealed to Aryan seers upon their conquering of northern India, issue the divine precepts, or *dharma*. The Avatāra rights that which the impious quantity upturns. Krishna continues: *In order to deliver the pious and to annihilate the miscreants, as well as to reestablish the principles of religion, I advent Myself millennium after millennium.*[2] The difference between God and man is potency: How much truth is present?

Truth reached its pinnacle in the life of Adolf Hitler; and as Hitler becomes more disparaged, more hated in the wake of his life, we see his struggle for what it was and is: the most recent and penultimate appearance of truth on earth. Adolf Hitler was the ninth Avatāra of the Godhead. He appeared in Germanic Europe when the godlessness of Judeo-capitalism and Judeo-Marxism were throwing the world into tumult. Britain, imbued with the "trader" spirit after generations of Jewish influence in the upper echelons of English society — a land of "Aryan bodies and Jew souls" who sit at "the center of the great conspiracy against the Aryans"[3] — was the main purveyor of Judeo-capitalism; Britain's colonial descendant and ascending partner, rife with Jewish agitator-capital after the "6 million" scares in Czarist Russia of the 19th and early 20th centuries,[4] was

---

[2] Bhagavad Gita, IV.8.

[3] See Werner Sombart's *Traders and Heroes: Patriotic Reflections*; Miguel Serrano's *Adolf Hitler: The Ultimate Avatar* (Hermitage Helm, 2014), 800; Miguel Serrano, *Manu: For the Man to Come* (Hermitage Helm, 2017), 188.

[4] See Thomas Dalton's *The Steep Climb* (2023) and Don Heddesheimer's *The First Holocaust*. 10 February 1889 (*New York Times*; hereafter *NYT*): "With the exception of half a million, they are all in a state of political bondage... [In] Russia alone there were 4,000,000 of their race whose every step was dogged by that curse, religious hatred and persecution." 26 January 1891 (*NYT*): "about six millions persecuted and miserable wretches remain steadfastly faithful to a religion that causes their life to be changed into a fiery furnace..." 11 June 1900 (*NYT*): "There are 6,000,000 living, bleeding, suffering arguments in favor of Zionism." 16 May 1903 (*NYT*): "We charge the Russian Government with responsibility for the Kishineff massacre. We say it steeped to the eyes in the guilt of

a looming Judeo-capitalist giant. Indeed, the Judeo-Anglo-American alliance pressed fervently for open conflict with the Germanic world:

> The British Establishment was more than eager to promise Palestine to the Jews of the world in exchange for a favor. Lord Balfour transacted the bargain: as a consideration for Jewish assistance in bringing America into the war on the British side, the government of Great Britain would deliver Palestine into Jewish hands once the war had been won. This British promissory note became known as the Balfour Declaration. Jewish assistance was indeed invaluable in reversing almost overnight America's entrenched neutralism. Suddenly Allied propaganda received full coverage in American newspapers. From 1917 the public was fed fantastic stories dressed up as news, such as the "discovery" that the Germans had secret gun emplacements in the United States ready to bombard New York and Washington. This alarming "news" had been planted by the Allies as early as October 1914 and had succeeded in finding its way into presidential intelligence reports... [Additionally, the] Lusitania gave the American press a field day. There was an explosion of journalistic out-

---

this holocaust." 10 November 1905 (*NYT*): "Simon Wolf asks how long the Russian holocaust is to continue." 23 March 1905 (*NYT*): "our 6,000,000 cringing brothers in Russia." 11 April 1910 (*NYT*): "Russian Jews in sad plight ... [over] the systematic, relentless, quiet grinding down of a people of more than 6,000,000 souls." 31 October 1911 (*NYT*): "the 6,000,000 Jews of Russia are singled out for systematic oppression..." 10 December 1911 (*NYT*): "the condition of the Jews in Russia is worse now than it ever was before... [T]he restrictive laws ... intensif[y] the oppression of ... the 6,000,000 Jews..." 1911 (*Herzl Year Book*, vol. 2, 156): "governments ... lay the groundwork with their own hands for the destruction of six million persons..." April 1920 (*NYT*): "typhus menaced 6,000,000 Jews of Europe." May 1920 (*NYT*): "Hunger, cold rags, desolation, disease, death — six million human beings without food, shelter, clothing." July 1921 (*NYT*): "Russia's 6,000,000 Jews are facing extermination by massacre." And so it goes, *ad nauseum*...

rage about the murder of innocent tourists. The massive press exploitation of these unfortunate passengers was decisive.... The Lusitania victims were combined with the stories of German gun emplacements in Brooklyn, the cutting off of Belgian children's hands and other barbarities. The Germans had now become *Teutons* and *Huns*. It took half a century to establish the truth about the Lusitania. An underwater exploration of the sunken ship revealed that its hulls were full of ammunition. The British arms dealers had used tourists to camouflage their war materiel. They had used twelve hundred lives to hide their contraband and collect their ill-gotten gains. The Germans were aware of this deception and were well within the bounds of international law by attacking an arms-carrying enemy vessel. The Lusitania was a warship disguised as an ocean liner by the British arms merchants. They lured twelve hundred innocent people to their deaths and they alone bear the guilt of this tragedy. As they unconscionably flew American flags on British ships to cover up their trafficking, so did they use innocent people.[5]

For its part, the Russian Revolution — almost wholly Jewish in nature[6] — midwifed a violent and bloody birth of the Soviet Union, a bastion of Judeo-Marxism, destroyer of the Germanic czarist lines, and fomenter of internationalist revolutions the world over. This, coupled with the Jewish "peace" of Versailles meant to crush the Germanic people forever, provided fertile ground for godless mate-

---

[5] Léon Degrelle, *Hitler, Born at Versailles*, ch. 31 & 32.
[6] See Rosenberg's *The Gravediggers of Russia* (1921). "[In] 1920, out of 380 Bolshevist commissaries, 300 were Jews.... The provinces are governed by 23 Commissaries, of which 20 are Jews.... Among the 42 dictators of the 'Russian' press there is only one who is *not* a Jew... The 'Russian' Soviet Government is made up of 34 Letts, 30 Russians, some Armenians, Poles, Czechs and 447 Jews! What better testimony is needed to show the Jewish character of the Bolshevist Movement?"

rialism, whose standard bearer was, first, the Soviet Republics of late- and postwar Germany,[7] then, the Weimar Republic. As Serrano reminds us:

> The First World War was provoked to destroy the last Central European monarchies, the German, Austrian and Czarist-Germanic. The Bolshevik Revolution is totally the work of Jews. The leaders and founders of socialism, of Marxism, of anarchism, are Jews. They destroyed Czarism and caused the triumph of the revolution of the Soviets in collaboration with the capitalism of Wall Street and the City with the economic empires of Baruch and the Rothchilds.[8]

God sees all, however, and provides haven for the harried, truth for the tormented. Yes, God sees all; thus, Hitler was born in the midst of this maelstrom.[9]

The truth of Hitler was his adherence to Nature; Nature, being the progenitor of all things, is divine. As the supreme representative of Nature's divine will, Hitler was more than a God-man; as

---

[7] Here are but a few of the (communist) Jews involved in revolutionary Germany: Rosa Luxemburg, Kurt Eisner, Paul Levi, Leo Jogiches, Ernst Toller, Erich Mühsam, Gustav Landauer, Eugen Leviné, Max Levin, Karl Radek, Karl Liebknecht, etc.

[8] Serrano, *Adolf Hitler: The Ultimate Avatar* (Hermitage Helm, 2014), 179.

[9] See again Degrelle's *Hitler, Born at Versailles*. Degrelle was a man of many talents and a great hero — a *hero* in the fullest sense of the word. A leader of Belgium's rising Rexist Party already by his mid-twenties, Degrelle resigned this path to volunteer for Hitler's *Schutzstaffel*, believing in the necessity of the Cosmic Struggle against Jehovahistic, satanic Marxism on Germany's Eastern Front. Fighting for several years on the front, Degrelle's heroism was awarded many times, sometimes by Hitler himself, who once said to him, "If I had a son, I would want him to be like you" (*Campaign in Russia* [Institute for Historical Review, 1989], 262). Degrelle survived the war, escaped extradition in Spain, and continued to fight for the Hitlerist cause in the postwar world. We revere his life and memory. "Born" is meant in Degrelle's sense, but extends beyond Versailles; God used Hitler's full life to communicate its will.

embodiment of the Germanic folk's will-to-live, he was God. His mission was divine consciousness and harmony with Nature.

Nature's divine will is elemental: earth, air, fire, water, and ether — these are the inanimate that make the animate. From these we must consider a sixth element: human spirit.[10] It is the nature of man that he carries on, that he overcomes, that he surmounts with spirit Nature's unrelenting drive to tear him apart. In this way, the sixth element is both beholden to the five inanimate elements and yet stands above them. Man is the paradox of Nature's diktat: overcome that which can never be overcome.

Man's ability to overcome resides in his character; character is a reflection of the soul, of the spirit. Character, likewise, is a concomitant to race, and "Race is the image of the soul."[11] Race, therefore, as mirror to the spirit, is just as aptly the sixth element. Race is the juncture of physical and spiritual, the confluence of inanimate and animate, the harbor of finite and infinite. Race is both the paradox and the explanation; we find in race our ability to overcome Nature and our absolute subjugation by Nature. Race is the key to understanding man's existence and achieving harmony with Nature; the sixth element is both *cosmos* and but a part of *cosmos*.

Adolf Hitler, as upholder of Nature's divine will, stands, therefore, as defender of truth. Both in his time and afterward, Hitler stood for the cause he knew would pit the world against him; for this, his life was the ultimate testament to bravery; his legacy, the symbol of heroic rectitude. His dharma was fulfilled, his purpose complete. God chooses the time and place of his manifestation as Avatāra. God chose Germany — *Gott mit uns* — because of the historical circumstances, because of the existential threat to an entire people. "If a nation has to fight a total war against half the world for its mere existence, ... a [warrior] community comes about on its

---

[10] The Bhagavad Gita instructs us on eight material energies: earth, air, fire, water, ether, mind, intelligence, and false ego (*ahankara*) (VII.4). Here I have combined the three human energies — mind, intelligence, and false ego — into one: *human spirit*.

[11] Alfred Rosenberg, *Myth of the Twentieth Century*. Also translated as "Race is the counterpart of soul." See *Myth* (Clemens & Blair, 2021), 20.

own."[12] The Germanic world, representing the last heroic spirit of an Aryan antiquity, was beleaguered for generations by alien agitation and influence because of its instincts of "warrior spirit" and "manly composure."[13] These instincts were its dharma, its necessity; in harmony with both God and Nature, these instincts drew the attention of the very best and very worst of man, of Good and Evil, and it culminated in the war against the Germanic people. This was not mere political struggle; this was not mere ideological conflict; the world's total war against the Germanic folk was a war of Good and Evil, a Cosmic Struggle of *quality* against *quantity*; it was the fight of the Supreme Creator against the Demiurge-Jehovah; it was the confrontation of Nature's creative will and the masses' automatized subservience — *this skirmish is not a capricious duel but a struggle under divine auspices.*[14] Adolf Hitler did not just defend the rights of the Germanic folk; he was the speaker for all men of quality, for all decency and creative spark, as is the case with every Avatāra. Hitler's struggle attracted support from across the world; in the end, the *Waffen-SS* represented a pan-European Army, and its ranks even extended to Asia, Africa, and South America — it was a force for all those who believed in fighting for God's will on earth. Indeed, one can look to the many "foreigners" found dead in Berlin's streets, having fought to the last to defend the Führer's struggle — the struggle for all men and women of quality. Savitri Devi, too, recounts of her stay in India:

> A boy of fifteen or so — [told] me ... : "I too, admire your Führer.... I admire him, and love him, because he is fighting to replace, in the West, the Bible by the Bhagavad-Gita." He had got that extraordinary piece of information from a talk in the Calcutta fish market.[15]

---

[12] Kurt Meyer, *Grenadiers* (Stackpole Books, 2001), 403.

[13] Meyer, *Grenadiers* (Stackpole Books, 2001), 403.

[14] Søren Kierkegaard, *Either/Or*, Part II (Princeton UP, 1987), translated by H. and E. Hong.

[15] *Gold in the Furnace* (Calcutta, 1952).

Adolf Hitler's fight for quality — *for* truth and *in* truth — transcends borders; so in a semblance of cosmic irony, Hitler's *völkisch* struggle was ultimately internationalist in character. It is mere *semblance*, however. For far from the Judeo-*materialism* that dominates and drives internationalism today, the Führer's "internationalism" was *spiritualism* — that is, the inner calling of a folk to its divine fate, the harmony of Nature and man. The harmony of Nature and man is a divine calling that resonates within the soul of every race. It is not a soulless economic construct of digitized decimals and integers, but a primeval communion that *feels* right, that *is* right for every divinely grounded people. Both Hitler and Goebbels were adamant:

> National Socialism confines itself to Germany and is not for export.... National Socialism absolutely places in the foreground of its program a belief in God and that transcendental idealism which has been destined by Nature to express the racial soul of a nation.[16]

Hitler's being, and therefore his program, was an expression of God in a German context, not unlike Krishna's encounter with Arjuna was expression of God in an early Aryan context. The appearance of God speaks to every man of quality, regardless of race. This is why the Führer's work was lauded even in the fish markets of Calcutta (Kolkata). In Western societies, it is only the "trader" (i.e., *traitor*) spirit — the spirit infected with godless, materialistic Jewishness — that disparages the National Socialist — or *Hitlerist* — program. And, as the most recent host to God's divine expression, the Germanic folk stands as deliverer of all quality remaining in the world. For the quality of the world to be freed of Jewish intrigues, all would have to recognize the inexorable will of the Germanic folk; for it is not the Germanic folk that is recognized, but God.

---

[16] Joseph Goebbels, "Communism With the Mask Off" (speech to the annual NSDAP Congress), 13 September 1935. Hitler, who no doubt ingrained this thought into Goebbels, reiterated this point in his speech of 20 May 1942 (*Hitler's Table Talk*).

The Avatāra appears to relieve us of our suffering; it is our choice whether or not to accept that which is revealed. One judges rightly when one sees a revelation as recovering elemental harmony. And in truth, a revelation stands as upright relative to our juxtaposition to it: proximity in space brings offense for those septic souls of Judaized slave-morality; proximity in time brings offense to those overwrought with waves of alien influence. The offense both reveals and obscures the revelation; as revelation, the offense unmasks those who would do the truth harm; as obscuration, the offense is an inability to adjudge the Avatāra because of a separation from God and the humanity that elevated our spirit to the heights of history. Separation is wrought of wreckage: erstwhile nobility of spirit is usurped for monetary machinations; Aryan spirituality is replaced with Jewish materiality. Separation is the absence of truth; hence it is that truth suffers in every generation.

∞ ∞ ∞

The purpose of this work is twofold: (1) examine the nature of Hitler's life as it stands in proximal time, and (2), by doing so, establishing the foundations for a future understanding of Hitler's life as its consequences become apparent and supreme in the light of faith — that is, as the consequences of Hitler's life are properly adjudged as correct and essential for the continued existence of mankind.

Achieving this end will require a study of:

- Hitler's own words regarding his purpose;
- The paradox of Hitler's life and the necessity of offense;
- The relationship of faith and reason;
- And the necessity of contemporaneousness for the faithful.

A needed prelude to the study, however, is a word on Judeo-Christianity — specifically, on its relation to Hitlerism. This prelude is vital (a) because of Hitler's appearance as Avatāra; to understand his appearance it is instructive to examine the appearance of Christ, which is readily understood by many folk of European descent, and

(b) because the preeminent spiritual investigation by any European mind is Kierkegaard's lifelong pursuit of a reckoning with faith, of which an interpretation of Christianity sat at the core. Kierkegaard's examination is foremost because it reintroduced *Germanic* — i.e., divine — *struggle* back into European Christendom. Prior to and contemporaneous with Kierkegaard, the institution of Christianity and, therefore, being a Christian had "become a thing of naught, mere tomfoolery, something which everyone is as a matter of course..."[17] Indeed, "all became as simple as thrusting a foot into the stocking"[18] — Christianity was nothing more than Asiatic, Levantine superstition; Christianity *is* nothing more than this. Kierkegaard recognized, in true Germanic fashion, that if faith is to have any meaning, it must be born of struggle; anything short of this is thoughtless, vapid exhalation, meant to distract unwitting pawns in a Jewish game.[19] Kierkegaard reminded Europe of its organic ethos.

∞ ∞ ∞

Our future will necessarily be receptive to the revelation of the Avatāra — this, or our future will not exist. This work stands as both a reflection of individual character and a revelation of the Aryan folk-soul; should one be abolished in the other through a lack of faith in our collective purpose, we forfeit any claim on viability. Extinction is our call to action. Faith is our salvation. And that which is done out of love always takes place beyond good and evil. Education is the key to understanding love. Love is the key to actions that will concretize the divine revolution. Turn your eyes to God and let faith be your educator; turn your eyes to faith and let Nature be your vengeance.

---

[17] Kierkegaard, *Training in Christianity* (Vintage, 2004), translated by Walter Lowrie, 61.

[18] Kierkegaard, *Training in Christianity* (Vintage, 2004), 30.

[19] Kierkegaard, whether he knew it or not, was a proponent of Germanicism, not Judeo-Christianity: Christianity can never move beyond mere Levantinism. Christianity is *meant* to be "mere tomfoolery" and superstition, like its concomitant *internationalism*, and unlike Germanicism, which is race-based and born of daily struggle.

Aryan vengeance means to restore the balance and rectitude of Nature; it is a reversal of Jewry's subversion of the divine order. The Jews' destructive urge, manifested in an *inversion of values*, has unraveled folk after folk, from the Palestinians to the Egyptians, and from the ancient Greeks and Romans to the Germanics. Nietzsche marked the Jews as

> a people "born for slavery," as Tacitus and the whole ancient world say of them; "the chosen people among the nations," as they themselves say and believe — the Jews performed the miracle of the inversion of valuations, by means of which life on earth obtained a new and dangerous charm ... [and] it is with *them* that the *slave-insurrection in morals* commences.[20]

Nietzsche describes radical, Jewish slave-morality as the *cleverest revenge*, which both reflects the Jewish nature and has defined their actions for millennia.

> It was the Jews who, in opposition to the aristocratic equation (good = aristocratic = beautiful = happy = loved by the gods), dared with a terrifying logic to suggest the contrary equation, and indeed to maintain with the teeth of the *most profound hatred* ... this contrary equation, namely, "the wretched are alone the good; the poor, the weak, the lowly, are alone the good..." It was, in fact, with the Jews that the *revolt of the slaves* begins in the sphere *of morals*; that revolt which has behind it a history of two millennia, and which at the present day has only moved out of our sight, because it — *has achieved victory*.[21]

Jews have achieved their ephemeral material victory through the imposition of their internationalist creeds: communism, atheism,

---

[20] Nietzsche, *Beyond Good and Evil*, §195.
[21] Nietzsche, *On the Genealogy of Morals*, Essay 1, §7.

scientism, international socialism, globalism, capitalism, human-ism, Christianity, etc. — that is, any creed that elevates a society's dregs or rejects the paramountcy of race in worldly and spiritual affairs. The Jewish inversion of values was and is the "most funda-mental of all *declarations of war*."[22] Yes, in their absolute *hatred* of Gentiles, the Jews have declared war! Jews are the *ferments of de-composition*[23] that have rotted culture after culture for their per-sonal and collective gain; they are exploiters of the ignorant, de-stroyers of the beautiful, and underminers of the strong — hence their attraction to and employment of the creeds that help them achieve these means to the ultimate end of Jewish supremacy over the callow and mongrelized masses.

Jewish vengeance has but one goal: Jewish supremacy. This vengeance is born of their Jehovah-god and its unquenchable lust for blood, especially that of non-Jews; hence we see Jewish med-dling in the background of every war, in the earmarks of every con-flict; hence we see heavy Jewish hands molding the vindictive ideo-logical standards of academia; hence we see Jewish influence stamped everywhere on the grotesqueries of the indoctrinating media industry.[24] Blood-soaked Jewish vengeance is the spiteful usurpation of the Divine Order of Nature for the sole benefit of Jews; Jewish supremacy is the reign of the Jews over a rootless and raceless international order. Nature, for the Jew, is merely another tool to pound into existence an enduring era of exploitation.

Aryan vengeance is the restoration of Nature's divine order, the righting of the Jewish wrong. Jews declared war on the Gentiles from the very beginning; we respond in kind. Aryans acknowledge "that compulsion can only be broken through compulsion, and ter-ror only by terror. Only then can a new order be created."[25] Only then will the "Jewish watchword *Proletarians of the world, unite!* ... be conquered by a far more lofty realization, namely: *Creative men of all nations, recognize your common foe!*"[26]

---

[22] Nietzsche, *On the Genealogy of Morals*, Essay 1, §7.
[23] Theodor Mommsen, *The History of Rome* (1856/1871), 643.
[24] See Thomas Dalton's "The Jewish Blood-Obsession" (Unz, 2023).
[25] Adolf Hitler, *Mein Kampf* vol. 2 (2019), 169; modified translation.
[26] Adolf Hitler, 30 January 1939 (speech).

— 1 —
Judeo-Christianity:
A Hitlerist Perspective

Hitler the man was "Christian" insofar as (1) Christianity was a rapport-building expedient in a nation predominantly Christian, and (2) he *somewhat* believed "Christ was an Aryan"[1] who fought against Jewish materialism and "set himself against Jewish capitalism, and that's why the Jews liquidated him."[2] This is to say that Hitler was not a Christian.

First, why *somewhat* believed? In *Mein Kampf*, Hitler states, "... the Christian marries a Jewess. The resulting mongrels *always fall on the Jewish side*. Thus a part of the higher nobility *becomes completely degenerate*."[3] This is significant because, according to Hitler, "It is quite probable that a large number of the descendants of Roman legionaries, mostly Gauls, were living in Galilee, and Jesus was probably one of them. His mother may well have been a Jewess."[4] Despite Jesus being "an Aryan" — i.e., if he existed at all, having, *at best*, half Roman blood — because Jesus' mother was Jewish, Hitler actually believed Jesus to be a "mongrel" and "completely degener-

---

[1] Adolf Hitler, 13 December 1941. This and some of the following quotes are from *Hitler's Table Talk* (*HTT*), an extensive collection of Hitler's informal utterings compiled by Martin Bormann, himself fiercely anti-Christian. Translations, no matter the topic or language, vary based on the translator; here is no different. While this or that translation of Bormann's collection might vary here or there, the essential content remains unchanged; regarding Christianity, Hitler's position was quite clear: Christianity was a stain on Europe and the Germanic folk that must be erased.

[2] *HTT*, 29 November 1944 and *HTT*, 21 October 1941.

[3] Adolf Hitler, *Mein Kampf* vol. 1 (Clemens & Blair, 2017), "Nation and Race," 583; emphasis added; in the note to this statement, editor T. Dalton rightly indicates, "... a Jewish woman bears Jewish children, even if the father is non-Jewish.... In Hitler's view, the Jewish (lower) half always prevails."

[4] *HTT*, 29 November 1944.

ate." Hitler respected Aryan (pre-Christian) Romans; on the other hand, Jews disgusted Hitler with their parasitism and degeneracy; despite the *remote* possibility that Jesus was part Roman, his blood — and therefore his soul — would have been *utterly corrupted*. Rather, what Hitler believed, and respected, about Jesus was his fight against Jewry. In this way, then, Hitler had *"feeling* as a Christian."[5] But Hitler was no Christian.

One cannot rise to the position of *leader* over a people whom one does not largely resemble. Christianity was part of Germany's national identity (because of its infiltration of Europe and subsequent absorption of Germanic characteristics); thus, Hitler must *resemble* his constituency, no matter if they are regular citizens, industrialists, or members of the military — many of whom were traditional Christians.[6] Despite his early feelings (and rhetorical pronouncements), Hitler was never keen on anything but the *Germanicism* he saw as "coloring" Christianity — Christianity was good because of its Germanic character.[7] It is worth taking a moment to explain this, as it will be a recurrent theme in this work. Georges Duby records that Christianity was an imposition upon northern Europeans and that, despite this, vestigial Germanicism informed what became European Christianity; he noted, "Pagan beliefs ... long persisted under the superficial guise of rites, tales and formulae imposed by force on the rest of the tribe by the converted chiefs."[8] Carl Erdmann puts it even more strongly:

---

[5] Adolf Hitler, 12 April 1922 (speech); emphasis added.

[6] And, while some were very capable men, it can be said with confidence that not many — those in the military, for example, with whom Hitler had a *strained* relationship, at best — could be accused of being deep thinkers.

[7] *HTT*, 27 September 1941. Christianity was nothing if not superimposed over the indigenous Germanic (pagan) beliefs permeating Europe. Aside from the sword, the only way to convince the Germanic people of Christianity's veracity was to liken it to preexisting traditions: One imagines what the early Christian missionaries might have said: "See, Jesus sacrificed himself just like Wotan did," "See, Jesus is strong just like Thor," "See, Jesus rose from the dead just as the northern sun does," and so on.

[8] Duby, *The Chivalrous Society* (UC Press, 1977), translated by Cynthia Postan, 216.

The moral precepts that accompanied [the Germanic people] from their pagan past were completely oriented to war, focusing on heroism, famous deeds on the part of the leader, loyalty on the part of the followers, revenge for those killed, courage unto death, contempt for a comfortable life at home. For them, war as such was a form of moral action, a higher type of life than peace. *All this stood at the opposite pole from Christian morality*, which is based on love and readiness for peace and can discuss war only with reference to aims and duties.... The church was therefore confronted with a massive barrier of pagan ways, which for centuries were beyond its power to master.... *When the church encountered pagan elements that it could not suppress, it tended to give them a Christian dimension, thereby assimilating them.* This happened to the ethics of [Germanic] heroism. The whole crusading movement may justifiably be seen from this perspective; Christian knighthood cannot otherwise be understood.[9]

We see here both the diametric opposition of the Judeo-Christian and Germanic ethics and the subsumption of Germanic traits into the Semitic religion to make it even remotely acceptable to coerced northern Europeans. Thus operating under such conditions, it was necessary for Hitler, to make his rhetoric palatable, to rationalize his appeals to himself — indeed, Hitler's alliance with the Judeo-Christian bloc was no different than his pact with Judeo-Bolshevism in 1939: it was expedient.[10]

---

[9] Erdmann, *The Origin of the Idea of Crusade* (Princeton UP, 1977), 19-20.
[10] Anyone who has ever had to build rapport with another from a different background can understand Hitler's position and approach; it makes complete sense. Regrettably, there yet exist many "National Socialist" or "Hitlerist" Christians. This can only be explained by provincialism: those who stubbornly hold on to the "Hitler was a Christian" view have likely never experienced the world outside their small community, and therefore have no conception of either *rhetoric* or *expedients*; they are also apparently unable to read or hear, for Hitler was, time and again, quite

Hitler was quite explicit in his interpretation of Christianity:

- "The heaviest blow that ever struck humanity was the coming of Christianity. Bolshevism is Christianity's illegitimate child. Both are inventions of the Jew." — 17 July 1941
- "The best thing is to let Christianity die a natural death." — 14 October 1941
- "Christianity is a prototype of Bolshevism: the mobilization of the masses by the Jew to undermine society." — 19 October 1941
- "Christianity was the invention of sick brains." — 13 December 1941
- "I don't believe [a synthesis between National Socialism and Christianity] is possible, and I see the obstacle in Christianity itself.... [Christianity] is merely wholehearted Bolshevism..." — 14 December 1941
- "Christianity is the worst regression that mankind has ever undergone..." — 20 February 1942
- "The Germanic races would have conquered the world. Christianity alone prevented them from doing so." — 28 August 1942
- "[National Socialism] is both anti-Communist and anti-Christian [because Communism and Christianity are Jewish institutions]." — 29 November 1944[11]

For those who wish to discount the authenticity of the above assertions, consider again *Mein Kampf*: "One may today regret the fact that the advent of Christianity marked the appearance of the first

---

clear about his stance on Christianity. (The preceding statement is not meant to malign small communities or simple living — each of these are valued. But Hitlerism — or any worthwhile living — can only be achieved with *thinking* people. It is *unthinkingness* that dismantles societies and is therefore the point of contention.)
[11] The foregoing statements are taken from *HTT*.

spiritual terror into the much freer ancient world."[12] Hitler's position is clear, and therefore establishes the *Hitlerist position* that the Germanic world was good *despite* Christianity, not because of it.[13]

Now, we know that Point 24 of the NSDAP's 25-Point Program attests to upholding "Positive Christianity, but does not bind itself in the matter of creed to any particular confession." That is, Hitlerism is not bound to any creed; it bears repeating: *Hitlerism is not bound to any religion.* This is because Hitlerism, revealed through the Avatāra, transcends mere religiosity, mere religion; it is *Nature-based diktat.* Circumventing or otherwise ignoring this diktat doesn't mean condemnation to a concocted New Testament hell — No! It means the extinction of your folk and Jewish enslavement for failure to fight to the end for the survival of your race; the stakes are far more serious, indeed; and Jewish enslavement does and will certainly mean new child sacrifices on the altars of Gehenna.[14] Further, Hitler — who was undoubtedly the main force behind and final arbiter of the 25 Points — declares "all religious denominations" subordinate to both the State *and* the Germanic race; let's say that again: *All religions are subordinate to both the State and the Germanic race.*[15] The preceding arguments should stultify any notions of "Christian National Socialism" or "Christian Hitlerism" — the positions *couldn't be more antithetical.* Nevertheless, one additional point on the 24th Point: Hitler's one-time deputy, Rudolf Hess, gave multiple speeches declaring that "Hitler is Germany and Germany is Hitler — whoever swears an oath to Hitler, swears an oath to

---

[12] Adolf Hitler, *Mein Kampf* vol. 2 (Clemens & Blair, 2019), "Worldview and Organization," 167.

[13] For more on this, see *Myth and Sun: Essays of the ARCHETYPE* (Clemens & Blair, 2022).

[14] Jeremiah 19. Far from abhorring such fiendish acts, the "God of Israel" (i.e., Satan, or Demiurge-Jehovah) craves such bloodthirsty sacrifice of non-Jewish innocents (see Toaff's *Passovers of Blood* [Clemens & Blair, 2020]). Gehenna will rise again with Jewish supremacy.

[15] The State is the formal representation of the folk (race), which is why it takes precedence in Hitler's Reich. For a detailed discussion of ethno-State philosophy, see *Myth and Sun: Essays of the ARCHETYPE* (Clemens & Blair, 2022).

Germany!"[16] Naturally, Hitler, as both Avatāra and Führer, approved of this testimony. If Hitler *is* the Program, if Hitler *is* the Movement, if Hitler *is* the State, if Hitler *is* the Nation[17] — then all creeds, confessions, and religions are subordinate to Adolf Hitler. This is only natural given Hitler's appearance as Avatāra and Führer.

We must also consider that Hitler surrounded himself with fervent *anti*-Christians or other expedient-minded *a*-Christians. Joseph Goebbels, Heinrich Himmler, Reinhard Heydrich, Alfred Rosenberg, Hermann Göring, Martin Bormann, Robert Ley — these are but a few of the non-Christians in Hitler's circle. Each of these men, like their Führer, shared an appreciation, be it implicit (spiritual) or explicit (intellectual), for the "great German philosopher,"[18] Friedrich Nietzsche. Nietzsche, of course, is quite known for his anti-Christian *Weltanschauung*, having even written the brilliant *Antichrist* (1888). Hitler's speeches are overflowing with Nietzschean sentiment, though the same cannot be said of any Christian attitude; strength through struggle — a *will-to-power* — is the essence of both Nietzschean and Hitlerian philosophy. Likewise, perusal of the extant speeches and writings of the men in Hitler's circle shows an overwhelming focus on Nietzschean *strength* and *struggle*, and an almost nonexistent accounting of *Christ* or *Christianity* (and the focus on the latter is nearly always negative).

Joseph Goebbels, with Hitler to the very end, was adamant that "being Christian means allowing the Jews to continue to rule."[19] Alfred Rosenberg — awarded the *Deutscher Nationalorden für Kunst und Wissenschaft* for his *Myth of the Twentieth Century*, which outlined the Myth of the Blood as superior to any Jewish

---

[16] The most famous of these proclamations came at the end of Riefenstahl's *Triumph des Willens* (1935), but another example is Hess' 25 February 1934 speech.

[17] For a detailed discussion of the *Führerprinzip*, which encapsulates this theme, see *Myth and Sun: Essays of the* ARCHETYPE (Clemens & Blair, 2022).

[18] Adolf Hitler, 30 January 1942 (speech). Hitler paraphrases Nietzsche's famous maxim: "A blow that does not knock a strong man over, only makes him stronger!"

[19] "Why Do We Oppose the Jews?" *Der Angriff*, 30 July 1928.

Christianity — observed that "Nordic self-awareness and Nordic racial discipline are the answer today to the Levantine east, which has diffused itself throughout Europe in the form of Jewry and varieties of ecumenicalism."[20] *Ecumenicalism*, of course, is direct reference to the Christian churches. The emphasis on "Nordic self-awareness and Nordic racial discipline," incidentally, was the crux of Rosenberg's "Positive Christianity," which is mentioned in the Party's 25-Point Program: "[Positive Christianity] consciously calls upon the Nordic blood to awaken," whereas the negative aspect morbidly focuses on Christ's death.[21] In short, "Positive Christianity" is euphemism for Nietzschean, Germanic *Volksglaube* — an *expedient* title given to a belief that little resembles Judeo-Christianity. Moreover, in his *Memoirs*, written shortly before his martyrdom at Nuremberg, Rosenberg recalled his "own persistent opposition to the churches and Christian dogma," and left this impression from his full and thoughtful life: "the [miscegenation] of the world [is] aided and abetted by Christianity." Rosenberg, too, quoted Heydrich as saying Christianity was an "antagonistic philosophy"[22] — *antagonistic* because of its evident Jewishness. "As for the Christian concept of God," the author of *Myth of the Twentieth Century* remembered of his Führer, "Hitler definitely rejected it in private conversations."[23]

Hermann Göring recorded that "[putting] 'vice' or 'next in rank' before Hitler's name was an absolute impossibility and was felt by all his followers to be an insult";[24] this perspective, again, seems fitting for the Avatāra; no one and nothing was above Hitler. Göring continues:

> We National Socialists believe that the Führer is simply *infallible* in all matters concerning the national and

---

[20] Alfred Rosenberg, *Myth of the Twentieth Century* (Clemens & Blair, 2021), 28.

[21] Rosenberg, *Myth* (Clemens & Blair, 2021), 60-61.

[22] *International Military Tribunal — Nuremberg*, vol. 11, 466, 16 April 1946.

[23] Rosenberg, *Memoirs*.

[24] *Germany Reborn* (1934), recounting Hitler's ascension to chancellor.

> social interests of the people.... It is something mysti-
> cal, inexpressible, almost incomprehensible which this
> unique man possesses, and he who cannot *feel* it in-
> stinctively cannot, in turn, *understand* it. We love
> Adolf Hitler — because we believe deeply and un-
> swervingly that God has sent him to save Germany.

It is appropriate to say Göring describes the religious (spiritual) ec-
stasy common among the enthusiastic faithful of many creeds. William James outlines it thusly:

> There is a state of mind, known to religious men, but
> to no others, in which the will to assert ourselves and
> hold our own has been displaced by a willingness to
> close our mouths and be as nothing in the floods and
> waterspouts of God. In this state of mind, what we
> most dreaded has become the habitation of our safety,
> and the hour of our moral death has turned into our
> spiritual birthday. The time for tension in our soul is
> over, and that of happy relaxation, of calm deep
> breathing, of an eternal present, with no discordant fu-
> ture to be anxious about, has arrived.... This enchant-
> ment ... is either there or not there for us.... Religious
> feeling is thus an absolute addition to the Subject's
> range of life. It gives him a new sphere of power. When
> the outward battle is lost, and the outer world disowns
> him, it redeems and vivifies an interior world which
> otherwise would be an empty waste.[25]

The anti-Christian feeling in Hitler's Program and among the Party
drivers was thus primal and intellectual: *intellectual* because they
saw the damage wrought by Jewish Christianity and strove against
it; *primal* because they felt the spiritual tug of God in their midst
and worked toward it. James, later in his *Varieties*, and fittingly,
quotes another Germanic thinker who describes what captures the

---

[25] *The Varieties of Religious Experience* (Penguin, 1985), 47-48.

cosmic-magnetism Hitler held over the Germanic folk and the world at large:

> The near presence of God's spirit may be experienced in its reality — indeed only experienced. And the mark by which the spirit's existence and nearness are made irrefutably clear to those who have ever had the experience is the utterly incomparable feeling of happiness which is connected with the nearness, and which is therefore not only a possible and altogether proper feeling for us to have here below, but is the best and most indispensable proof of God's reality. No other proof is equally convincing, and therefore happiness is the point from which every efficacious new theology should start.[26]

This feeling supplanted Judeo-Christianity among the considerate in Hitler's Germany, and it underlies Hitlerism today.

Heinrich Himmler, as *Reichsführer-SS*, reoriented the ablest Germanics (represented in the SS) back to their Germanic roots. Organization publications like *Die Gestaltung der Feste im Jahres und Lebenslauf in der SS-Familie*[27] gave voice to old traditions, plainly contravening the Judeo-Christian church:

> The Christian church chose [Easter] this ancient Germanic feast of reawakening and resurrection for its celebration of the resurrection of the Christ. Easter is the feast of the victorious Spring during which the law of the eternal life of Nature is visible in the thousands of buds and growing seeds around us. These days of Easter are celebrated by the Germanic man by gathering round the Easter Fire, the Tree of Life in the house, willow catkins, Easter Eggs and the festive meal. Be-

---

[26] *Varieties* (Penguin, 1985), quoting Carl Hilty, 79.
[27] *The Structure of Celebrations in the Year and Life of the SS-Family* (1939).

cause he sees God's revelation in the laws of Nature, all these symbols are signs of his closeness to God.[28]

The SS was founded as the personal guard of Hitler; it had morphed into the bastion of Hitlerism, both domestically (*Allgemeine-SS*) and abroad (*Waffen-SS*). The SS was, in fact, based on the old Germanic bond between a leader and his retinue:

> Both prestige and power depend on being continually attended by a large train of picked young warriors, which is a distinction in peace and a protection in war. And it is not only in a chief's own nation that the superior number and quality of his retainers bring him glory and renown. Neighboring states honor them also, courting them with embassies and complimenting them with presents. Very often the mere reputation of such men will virtually decide the issue of a war.[29]

Had the Judeo-Anglo-American-Soviet juggernaut (*quantity*) not interfered and Hitler's Reich had time to develop, the SS would have moved from *elite group* to simply *the norm*; this was the intent, after all: a reestablishing of the aboriginal, pre-Christian arc of the Germanic folk. Hitler's SS was to be a foundational organization of the New Order, the divine order of Nature — built upon joy and love for one's folk. Unsurprisingly, it was an organization shorn of Judeo-Christian — and destructively hateful — sensibility.

Robert Ley, the last of Hitler's circle to be cited here, summed up our discussion quite nicely: "God Jehovah, God of Vengeance — he will devour you!" This, of course, encapsulates the Jewish (and Judeo-Christian) *will-to-devour* all things noble, decent, and honorable.

Nobility, decency, and honor were all signified in the Aryan Swastika — the indelible sign Hitler chose for the Movement. Da-

---

[28] Authored by *SS-Obergruppenführer* Fritz Weitzel, translated by Charles Barger (2007).
[29] Tacitus, *Germania*.

ting back to the earliest history, swastikas were diffused throughout the world, likely on the spiritual-cultural (i.e., racial) wave accompanying the ancient Aryans.[30] *Das Hakenkreuz* is the sign of the sun, the sign of Germanic will, the sign of God. Thus it was chosen by the Avatāra for his Movement; thus it was presented with inscriptions to Wotan in pre-Christian Europe.

(Image credit: Arnold Mikkelsen, National Museum of Denmark)

As Guido von List observed, "the greatest care was taken to conceal [the Swastika] as much as possible [in European heraldry] in order to make it appear more like the Christian cross"; hence the existence of the German Cross.[31] The vestiges of pre-Christian Europeans had to disguise their allegiance to the Aryan Swastika when the Jewish desert religion infiltrated northern lands, lest they and their families be converted with the sword. This allegiance was lost, however, among the imperial-papal crusades, the Hanse, and the bloodless machinations of meritless aristocracies — fertile ground for the Jew. And, so, *das Hakenkreuz* became the Cross; the Aryan became enslaved.

Finally, we have to wonder why (and how) any supporter of Hitler could possibly be a Christian, given Jesus' *Jewishness*. This

---

[30] For more on this, see *Myth and Sun: Essays of the ARCHETYPE* (Clemens & Blair, 2022).

[31] Guido von List, *The Secret of the Runes* (1914). See also *Myth and Sun: Essays of the ARCHETYPE* (Clemens & Blair, 2022).

point was alluded to above, but it bears reviewing. It is worth high-lighting a few examples of more recent Christological scholarship. Richard Rubenstein flatly states: "Jesus was a Jew."[32] A Jew himself, Rubenstein would seemingly have more interest in arguing the opposite, given the "anti-Semitic" furor levied against Jews in Jesus' name: it would be simply one more chance to play the victim — as Jews are wont to do — if Jesus were a proud Aryan. Two Christian scholars offer their stark assessment of Jesus: "Jesus was a Jewish mystic" (Marcus Borg) and "Jesus was a first-century Palestinian Jew" (N. T. Wright).[33] Christianity is fundamentally Jewish and, if Jesus existed at all, he was certainly a Jew — even half Jewish, according to Hitler. Thus, Christianity, in all its superimposition over Germanic culture, has nothing whatsoever to do with Germanicism and Hitlerism.

The alien creed of Christianity, with its liberalizing Jewishness, never was and cannot be congruent with Germanicism — i.e., being Germanic or Aryan. The *notion*, let alone the *reality*, of a "conservative" or, better, traditionalist Christian is *impossible*. Christianity either ignores or is hostile to the essentialness of race, and race serves as the bedrock of every close-knit, culture-spawning community in history; genuine, or *spiritual*, conservatism (or traditionalism) is concerned with preserving the familial-communal characteristics of a folk; these traits arise out of the racial stock; thus, ignoring or combating the essentialness of race precludes the conservation of the characteristics of a community. Christianity took root in a decaying Roman society that lost its folk-foundation:

> Not only was Roman family solidarity in a state of decline during the expansion of Christianity in the third and fourth centuries, but national solidarity was also waning... One of the greatest appeals of the Christian Church in a socially disintegrating Roman Empire was its role as an alternative community...[34]

---

[32] *When Jesus Became God* (Harcourt, 1999), xiv.
[33] *The Meaning of Jesus* (HarperCollins, 2000), 60 & 31, respectively.
[34] James C. Russell, *The Germanization of Early Medieval Christianity* (Oxford UP, 1994), 127-128.

We might think of Christianity as the fungus decomposing the dying tree of a once great Roman folk-community. The alternative Christian community provided solace to a people set adrift by a Semiticized Rome. But Roman society's degenerative effects of the neglect of their familial foundation could not be assuaged by an equally degenerative Christianity.[35] A fungus will never be a mighty oak.

Internationalist in scope and obsessed with the absurdities of "god's children" and a "brotherhood of man," Judeo-Christianity was a comforting veneer more inimical than even Roman society's shift from a spiritual-aristocracy to its empire-at-all-costs material-aristocracy — more inimical because it *internationalized* the sense of community, which is to say it formulated the dismantling of traditional communities. Jehovah is as inimically internationalist as the Judaized golems worshipping it — geographic and racial borders ceased to exist because the Judeo-Christian god recognizes no borders. However, nothing could be further from Germanic sense of truth. The very nature of Germanicism is reflected in the strong familial — i.e., *racial* — bonds of Germanic communities. "The notion of Christian honor, with its goal of individual salvation, directly opposed the supremacy of the Germanic concept of *vridu*, the bond of kinship which could be extended to others through an oath of loyalty..."[36] Moreover,

> Kindred was the foundation of [Indo-European] concentric structure, grouping the families in clans, claiming descent from a common ancestor, and the clans in

---

[35] From Russell, *The Germanization of Early Medieval Christianity* (Oxford UP, 1994), 128: "Valentinian 'expressly enacted that "no Roman citizen should be compelled to serve," except for the defense of his town in case of danger.' [As Robert M. Adams noted]: 'This indeed is the simplest definition of decadence; it is not failure, misfortune, or weakness, but deliberate neglect of the essentials of self-preservation — incapacity or unwillingness to face a clear and present danger.'" On the contrary, *deliberate neglect* can only be described as *failure*, for such neglect is both cause and symptom of societal collapse — i.e., *failure*.
[36] Russell, *The Germanization of Early Medieval Christianity* (Oxford UP, 1994), 121.

> tribes, presumably deriving their origin from some
> eponymous ancestor. Ethnic solidarity became espe-
> cially manifest in contrast with outsiders.... Inside his
> group, with his kith and kin, the Indo-European is safe;
> outside lurk the dangers. Inside his family, his clan, his
> tribe, he enjoys all the rights and privileges that per-
> tain to free members of the community.[37]

But it is precisely this *outside* that Judeo-Christianity introduces
inside the folk. And thus begins the *ferment of decomposition.*

The absolute and unbridgeable gulf between Germanicism and
Christianity is captured in a satire of Christ's Sermon on the Mount
(Matthew 5:3-12), which illustrates the Germanic perspective:

> Blessed are the rich, for they possess the earth and its
> glory. Blessed are the strong, for they can conquer
> kingdoms. Blessed are they with strong kinsmen, for
> they shall find help. Blessed are the warlike, for they
> shall win wealth and renown. Blessed are they who
> keep their faith, for they shall be honored. Blessed are
> they who are open handed, for they shall have friends
> and fame. Blessed are they who wreak vengeance, for
> they shall be offended no more, and they shall have
> honor and glory all the days of their life and eternal
> fame in ages to come.[38]

The Germanic focus is on the personal and familial glory that
comes from strength and honor. This stands in stark contrast to the
usual Christian preoccupation with world-hate, which translates
into disregard of the clan, and meek death for individual "salvation." We see here a difference in attitude between the Christian
and Germanic: The Germanic inclination is *individualistic with regard to the community* — that is, the Aryan esteems personal free-

---

[37] Edgar Polomé, ed., *The Indo-Europeans in the Fourth and Third Millennia* (Karoma, 1982), 161-167.
[38] George Jones, *Honor in German Literature* (UNC Press, 1959), 40-41.

dom because it means his clan's freedom; the Christian attitude, on the other hand, *focuses selfishly on the individual for the individual's sake* — what happens to the community beyond the individual's salvation is concern only for the individuals within said community. And while there is merit to the inward struggle an individual must undergo for the sake of authenticity, as is discussed below, this struggle must prelude and reflect the loftier fight for the individual's folk; if the individual's purpose is not a means to the transcendent folk-purpose, then we are left with the individual's purpose being an end in itself, which is to say, we are left with the liberalistic, race-killing attitude. This dichotomy is even seen in how Christianity manifested among Germanic northern Europeans after it was forcibly imposed: "the Mediterranean hermits fight more interior battles against their flesh, against demons who attack their perceptions, and they are 'slaves of God' in undertaking these combats; while the northern hermits, on the other hand, fight more concrete external opponents, are more literal soldiers, and are hailed as 'men of God.'" The Germanic northerners, despite the Christian missionaries' attempts, could not and would not, as freedom-loving people, completely shed their Aryan lifeways, of which being a warrior for the community played the major role.[39]

> The centrality of the warrior figure to the Indo-European and hence Germanic ethos ... [emanates from] the "*Männerbund*, organized around the person of a fearless leader [a Führer], [which] seems to have been the 'secret weapon' that facilitated the [Indo-

---

[39] James Russell, *The Germanization of Early Medieval Christianity* (UNC Press, 1994), 125 (preceding quote), and from p. 118 of the same text: "[Medieval] European society ... though professing belief in a religious system having its roots in the Semitic tradition, was nevertheless an I-E [Indo-European] speaking one and, as such, heir to the common I-E ideology." We note the "fundamental similarity in the ideological and sometimes the social structure among the ancient societies of India, Persia, Greece, Rome, and pre-Christian northern-Europe" (Russell, citing Dumézil's comparative model of Indo-European societies, 107).

European] expansion. The warrior was thus the prop
and ... pivot of the social system."[40]

With Jewish Christianity — born of a conquered, internationalist
people in Aryan Rome with its intended purpose of undermining
and dismantling the warrior ethos that supported the larger Aryan
community — the seeds of the self-obsessed, liberalistic attitude
are indeed sown. Adolf Hitler, as Führer and Avatāra of freedom-
loving Aryans, lived to expunge this Jewish neurosis from the Germanic folk and return Nature to the center of Aryan being.

Adolf Hitler was the embodiment of the Germanic will and
unmasked, *for all time*, the Eternal Enemy of the Aryan folk: the
International Jew. The Jew uses every conceivable scheme to infil-
trate and usurp Aryan lifeways for the latter's enslavement, which is
meant to support Jewish supremacy. Judeo-Christianity is but one
of the deceptions Jews have used to penetrate Aryan cultures and
generate the mass liberalistic, guilt-based psychosis that facilitates
the crippling self-harm, if not the racial suicide, folk of European
descent endure and inflict. One could offer example after example
of the diametric opposition of Germanicism — of *Hitlerism* — and
Judeo-Christianity; the evidence is ample, but the abovementioned
clues suffice to set the stage for the remainder of the present work.
The purpose of this section was to understand Hitler's oppositional
posture toward Judeo-Christianity *qua* Avatāra, which, in the context of Kierkegaard's preeminent study of faith, was a necessary
step to clear the path of *understanding faith* of any pitfalls.

---

[40] Russell, *The Germanization of Early Medieval Christianity* [UNC Press,
1994], 117 — this quote includes Russell's citation of Scott Littleton's *The
New Comparative Mythology* (1982).

Hitler: Der Sprecher des Rechts

Hitler saw himself as, foremost, a *speaker*. Speech galvanizes the latent powers of the collective unconscious, *the memory of the blood*. From this latency arises an omnipotent will-to-create — it needs only coaxing to bring it to light. Hitler possessed the ability to charm the will of his folk because the will of his folk possessed *him*. "I am the speech of them that speak," proclaims the Führer, and the path to enlightenment is revealed.[1] From clear speech comes natural conclusions; the Avatāra alone is conclusive. Hitler's Reich *was* the Nietzschean *Übermensch*.[2] Extending even beyond the political and geographical borders of temporality, the Reich's borders found anchor in the Blood Memory of all who yearn for the Natural Law of Divine Right. "For who am I?" asks the Führer, "I am nothing other than your *speaker* — the *speaker for your rights!*"[3] The merging of Reich, folk, and Führer cast the spell of conclusiveness *for all time*. Nietzsche's *Übermensch* reached fulfillment in the body of a people in harmony with Natural Law.

Hitler was not mere speaker. His thoughts and will are recorded for those compassionate souls who burn for the divine spark.

> My writing is not for strangers. I know ... that every great movement in this world owes its growth to great speakers, not to great writers. Still, writing is necessary

---

[1] Bhagavad Gita, X.32, translated by Franklin Edgerton.

[2] Contrary to what the Jews and their Shabbos-academicians would have us believe, the *Übermensch* was never a mere man; it was always meant as the collective will of a people. The Jew will never understand Aryan thought — a prime example: Walter Kaufmann's translation and editorializing of Nietzsche's work. For more on this, see *Myth and Sun: Essays of the ARCHETYPE* (Clemens & Blair, 2022).

[3] 30 January 1940 (speech).

to create a unified teaching we can distribute. I must
lay down its principles for all time.[4]

For all time — this is the goal of every divine incarnation. Work of
the Avatāra is coextensive with the infinite. The finite unbounded
is the infinite; the Avatāra unbounded is the Paradox. Principles
laid down are necessary for reminders of the Divine and they inspire future generations; yet "the moment [great ideas] enter the
realm of this life of sin, of the *all-too-human*, they leave the heavens
and lose their romantic magic."[5] The Avatāra unbounded is the will
of God to express itself in the finite; success here comes from the
communion of finite and infinite in the will of the Avatāra.

Hitler speaks for those with *long ears*; he writes for a time that
was and will be, but never is. "What hidden wisdom it is to wear
long ears, and only to say *Yea* and never *Nay!*"[6] We see what contempt the naysayers have for Hitlerism. Their hate is our joy — for
when evildoers hate you, rest assured that your path is correct, and
there is joy in truth; and "happiness is the point from which every
efficacious new theology should start."

Christ was crucified by the Jews — by Paul, alone[7] or with his
Pharisaic friends; Christ stole the joy of Germanic Easter, Germanic
Yule, Germanic sacrifice, and these fertile fields were overplanted
with short ears that miss the message. Conversely, Wotan freely
gave his life for the secret of the runes — so long ears would have
words to hear. Hitler, too, faced a world full of enemies and *nonetheless* earned victory through honorable sacrifice. Joy is yet alive in
the words, spoken or written: Let your joy be a *nonetheless*.

∞ ∞ ∞

––––––––––––––––––

[4] From the foreword of later editions of *Mein Kampf*.
[5] Joseph Goebbels, "Knowledge and Propaganda," 09 January 1928 —
echoing Nietzsche and even Max Weber.
[6] Friedrich Nietzsche, *Thus Spoke Zarathustra*, translated by Thomas
Common, Part IV, "The Awakening."
[7] See Thomas Dalton's *The Steep Climb* and David Skrbina's *The Jesus
Hoax* for more on this.

It is no coincidence that Hitler's favorite subjects were history and geography.[8] These fields are the juncture of humanity, and one informs the other: *Blut und Boden*, blood and soil. Their intersection spawned geopolitics, a field pioneered by Karl Haushofer. Haushofer mentored both Hitler and Hess during their stay at Landsberg. The teacher was to become the student, however, as the Führer came to embody geopolitics, and Haushofer became a pillorying pensioner. Postwar Haushofer displayed the delicate dance of distancing: *His ideas weren't mine!* If only the Haushofers would have been sincere in their attempts to help salvage the Reich through Hitler's earnestly sought peace via the Duke of Hamilton. It was all charade, however; Seydlitzes and Canarises lurk around every corner, and Churchill had to pay his dues to the Jews. Geopolitics became generally accepted after Hitler so deftly employed it — *distance and demonize, but do it nonetheless*, so say his detractors. They can detract, but they cannot demolish, despite their efforts. The Avatāra is eternal; geopolitics — blood and soil — is Aryan *Esperanto*.[9]

As he reflected later in life, Hitler noted two important inflections that began to affect his *Weltanschauung* during his pivotal stay in Wien: "First, I became a nationalist. Second, I learned to understand and grasp the true meaning of history."[10] *Nationalist*, of course, means *racialist*, or one who upholds the Natural Law. Before our Judeo-Anglo-American-Soviet era, *nation* meant a collection of *kinsmen*, born of the same blood, sharers of a common view of past, present, and future. Now, *nation* can mean as little as *speakers-of-the-same-language*: Welcome to the age of the non-German German, where every European nation aspires to the generic commercialism of Judeo-America — so long as they speak the

---

[8] *Mein Kampf* vol. 1 (Clemens & Blair, 2017), "In My Parents' House," 55.

[9] Esperanto is the "international" language created by the Jew Ludwik Zamenhof, who happened to believe in "a world without ... war" (Gabriela Zalewska, *Ludwik Zamenhof*, YIVO Encyclopedia of Jews in Eastern Europe [2014]). Just as Jews are eternally enthralled with the *international*, the Aryan — in diametric opposition — is born for, and *speaks*, the *national*, blood and soil.

[10] *Mein Kampf* vol. 1 (Clemens & Blair, 2017), "In My Parents' House," 55.

same language, or maybe just so long as they produce and consume without disruption. How vapid. Hitler, then, became a nationalist in the *real* sense of the word. As for grasping the "true meaning of history," this is Hitler's recognition of the manipulation and the manipulators: Jews as the perennial agitators, perpetual subverters, and fast fearmongers. "FEAR — is an exception with us. Courage, however, and adventure, and delight in the uncertain, in the unattempted — COURAGE seemeth to me the entire primitive history of man."[11] Hitler understood the primitive history of man: *race* and *courage*. We must have the courage to uphold the blood of our ancestors; we must have courage to stand aright in the face of constant attack from those who seek to eradicate our lineage, Nature's diktat. And though our lot in life seems to be a harsh one, with the Goddess of Fate taking us in her arms, threatening to smash us, we remain firm, our spirit growing stronger, our eyes fixed on the will meant to carry us through. The Avatāra sets the example.[12]

During his time in Wien, Hitler recognized the threat of both Judeo-Marxism and Judeo-capitalism, two sides of the same Jewish coin devised and deployed to dismantle Aryan lifeways and enslave the masses in a *brave new world*[13] where nearly all are drugged and distracted: "namely [Hitler saw] that, under the cloak of social virtue and love of one's neighbor, a veritable pestilence was spreading abroad, and that if this pestilence were not immediately stamped out, it might result in the end of the human race on earth."[14] In the wake of the Judeo-Anglo-American-Soviet war on the Avatāra, the

---

[11] Nietzsche, *Thus Spoke Zarathustra*, translated by Thomas Common, Part IV, "Science."

[12] *Mein Kampf* vol. 1 (Clemens & Blair, 2017), "Years of Studying and Suffering in Vienna," 73.

[13] Huxley's *Brave New World* is often overlooked for Orwell's *1984*; both stories, however, are equally predictive of the current (and growing) dystopia. Psychological manipulation, drugging, distracting — all work together to keep the masses from seeing the malefactors. Augustine of Hippo once remarked, "He is freely in bondage who does with pleasure the will of his master" (*Enchiridion*). This state of affairs exists today, all by design.

[14] *Mein Kampf* vol. 1 (Clemens & Blair, 2017), "Years of Studying and Suffering in Vienna," 105.

pestilence is now endemic, and humanity's days are numbered. Certainly the days of the postwar order are limited, for it is built upon Jewish slave-morality, which is pernicious and anti-Nature:

> It was, in fact, with the Jews that the *revolt of the slaves* begins in the sphere of *morals*; that revolt ... has achieved victory.... [For] it was the Jews who [stood] in opposition to the aristocratic equation (good = aristocratic = beautiful = happy = loved by the gods) [and it was] the Jews, [who effected] a radical transvaluation of values, which was at the same time an act of the *cleverest revenge*.[15]

The *aristocratic equation* is the harmony with Nature sought by the Avatāra. *Aristocratic* here does not refer to banal hereditary titles, but rather the noble nature of decent folk — nobility of character, mind, build, and being. Before *nobility of being* (spiritual, uncommon today) became *nobility of society* (material, all-too-common today), one rose to the highest ranks because of merit. The king was king because he was the best of his people; the knight was lord because he proved himself again and again. Unlike today when nominal leaders simply command their people to fight foreign wars for the benefit of shadowy coffers and blithely observe from afar, the nobility of yore led the way in these battles, they lived and died with their folk — and it must be emphasized that this has as much metaphorical meaning as it does literal meaning. The difference between a spiritual-aristocracy and a material-aristocracy is *empire*. Jews, as creators and purveyors of subversive slave-morality, crave material empire (having no notion of *the spiritual* themselves). Slave-morality is their means of establishing empire.

Nietzsche's reference to the "revolt of the slaves" recalls the gradual decay of the Roman occupation of extra-European lands — in this case, the Levant — through the insidious workings of their subjects. The decay of Roman occupation, of course, became the decay of the Roman Empire. Empire increases wealth in proportion

---

[15] *On the Genealogy of Morals*, translated by Horace Samuel, Essay 1, §7.

to a decrease in health; that is, the imperial wars of a healthy nation which sacrifice much good blood and expand the wealth of a nation (through the expansion of borders or influence) make necessary an opening of national "borders" from non-indigenous stock to replenish that which was lost in expeditionary, material expansion; the folk become exhausted, lose their communal focus, and become fodder for ever more imperialistic aims. A materialistic mindset must precede empire, and this is concurrent with the shift from spiritual-aristocracy to material-aristocracy; this aristocratic shift also cultivates the loss of communal focus through subsections of society. Before imperial wars (and thus the expansion of empire), the once inward-looking folk turn their gaze to interests beyond their nation (i.e., their blood); this is to say that *national* foci become *international*. It is precisely this reason that Hitler despised the Hapsburgs: "If the Parliament was worthless, the Hapsburgs were worse,"[16] for here was an outmoded, decrepit aristocracy that saw nothing of spiritual value — it sacrificed health for wealth; it ended its existence with neither health nor wealth, however.

Many an empire has and will go the way of the Greeks, the Romans, and the Hapsburgs. Jews agitate for revolution from above and below; since the beginning of recorded history, Jewish advisors with royal audiences have poured the profit-poison into ambitious Aryan ears — Jewry here sought windfalls from regional and expeditionary (or international) destabilization; since the beginning of recorded history, Jewish zealots or Jewish-funded rabble-rousers have seeped root-rotting, "power to the people" promises to the masses, getting them to doubt the traditions that granted them life — Jewry here sought windfalls from domestic destabilization. In both cases we have the hallmarks of Jewish slave-morality: Jews work from above to de-spiritualize the aristocracy, upending ancestral nobility and the drive for blood-bound merit; Jews work from below to devalue and debase all that was and is beautiful and good, all in the name of "social virtue" and "love of one's neighbor." Values are utterly upturned; people become drones and ripe for Jewish

---

[16] *Mein Kampf* vol. 1 (Clemens & Blair, 2017), "General Political Reflections from My Time in Vienna," 177.

rule. Jews often work in tandem — from above and below — to maximize monetary and societal profit. Formerly, dynastic empires, decayed from generations of waxing materialistic forces and expansions, were the Jews' currency; presently, "liberal-democracies" the world over rely on fiat currency, autonomous banking powers, tried-and-true colonial practices (installing desired minorities in official positions), Marxist doublespeak, technocratic cultism, subversive funding and money laundering masked as *philanthropy*, and media-academic-algorithmic indoctrination to distract the masses from Jewish intrigues; Jews have remarkable "ability to turn public attention away from [their actions]..."[17] The end result is always the same: Aryan values are dragged through the muck; Aryans succumb to depravity; Jews gain the world — parasitic maneuvering complete. But the world is not the goal, and Jewish power is fleeting.

Perhaps nowhere else does Adolf Hitler explain both the fundamental problem facing this world and his mission as Avatāra more clearly than in this passage from *Mein Kampf*:

> The Jewish doctrine of Marxism rejects the aristocratic principle of Nature, substituting for it ... numerical mass and dead weight. Thus it denies the individual value of the human personality, and impugns the idea that nationhood and race have primary significance. In doing so, it takes away the very foundations of existence and culture. If this doctrine were ever accepted as the foundation of the universe, it would lead to the disappearance of all conceivable order. Adopting such a law would provoke chaos in the structure of the greatest organism that we know — and the inhabitants of this earth would vanish. If the Jew, with the aid of his Marxist creed, were to triumph over the people of this world, his crown will be the funeral wreath of mankind. And this planet will once again follow its orbit through the ether devoid of humanity, just as it did

---

[17] *Mein Kampf* vol. 2 (Clemens & Blair, 2019), "The Mask of Federalism," 363.

> millions of years ago. Eternal Nature inevitably avenges those who violate her commands. Hence today I believe that I am acting in accordance with the will of the Almighty Creator: In defending myself against the Jew, I am fighting for the work of the Lord.[18]

Thus the problem and solution are captured, in written form, *for all time.* "In order to deliver the pious and to annihilate the miscreants, as well as to reestablish the principles of religion, I advent Myself millennium after millennium," thus spoke the Avatāra.[19] Even if books and language were to pass into oblivion, the will of Eternal Nature would still be branded in our being — there is no escaping it; that the divine will of Nature should ever be desired to be circumvented or obliterated is only a sign of our darkest of ages, the Kali-Yuga. "The whole cosmic order is under Me," spoke the Supreme Creator, and "By My will it is manifested again and again, and by My will it is annihilated at the end."[20] Hitler the man was the vessel for God; his life and work, because it was part of the Cosmic Order, was yet subordinated to God; thus we see (a) the Paradox and (b) the offense: (a) If he is an historical person, the Avatāra ceases to be an object of faith — the Avatāra ceases to exist; yet if the Avatāra exists, he was never an historical person; (b) Proximity in space brings offense for those septic souls of Judeo-slave-morality; proximity in time brings offense to those overwrought with waves of alien influence. The offense both reveals and obscures the revelation; as revelation, the offense unmasks those who would do the truth harm; as obscuration, the offense is an inability to adjudge the Avatāra because of a separation from God and the humanity that elevated our spirit to the heights of history.

We know the Paradox exists because we know the Godhead exists; we know the Godhead exists because we see it manifested in history — *in history*, but not as an historical being; God is written in our being as that which *stands for* quality and decency and

---

[18] *Mein Kampf* vol. 1 (Clemens & Blair, 2017), "Years of Studying and Suffering in Vienna," 153.
[19] Bhagavad Gita, IV.8.
[20] Bhagavad Gita, IX.8.

stands against the rising tide of mass depravity, which threatens to undermine Eternal Nature, the Cosmic Order. Such depravity is elicited when "women are corrupted [and the] mixture of caste ensues," which "leads to naught but hell."[21] The Avatāra is the appearance of that which stands *above* the Cosmic Order *within* the Cosmic Order. The Cosmic Order cannot be an historical being any more than a Darwinian "monkey mind" can begin to understand the evolutionary processes that supposedly gave it consciousness.[22]

------

[21] Bhagavad Gita, I.41-42, Edgerton translation. While this translation is preferred because of its evocativeness, Edgerton here renders *varna-sankara* as "caste." It should be noted, however, that when Krishna Avatāra speaks of castes mixing, he means the mixing of *varnas*, which are based on the *gunas*. A *guna*, as an aspect of material nature (*aparā-pakriti*), can have the character of ignorance (*tamas*), passion (*rajas*), or goodness (*sattva*). What became the caste system was based initially upon *varna*, which is to say, based upon *character*; this system was installed by the Aryans. (*Aryan*, recall, is derived from the Sanskrit *ārya*, meaning "noble.") Race, as a reflection of the soul, or one's character, was historically used as a means to assess character — because race demonstrated the rule; that is, one's race was reflective of one's character, which largely still holds to this day. Thus a hierarchy based on race and character (*varna*) became a hierarchy based solely on race (*caste*); this mirrors the shift in Europe from the spiritual-aristocracy to the material- or hereditary-aristocracy. Or, that which was once good became distorted and lost over time — because of weakness in character. Nonetheless, the original incarnation of the *varna-castes* amounted to fair, noble Aryans at the top, and dark, ignoble Sudras at the bottom. Thus when Alfred Rosenberg presents a brief history of *varna* in his *Myth of the Twentieth Century*, the spirit of his meaning is correct: "When the first great Nordic wave rolled over the high mountains into India, it had already passed through many hostile races. Almost instinctively, the Indo-Aryans separated themselves from the dark alien peoples they encountered. The caste institution was the outcome of this instinctive aversion. 'Varna' means caste, but it also means color. The fair Aryans thus linked themselves to an acceptable image of the human type, and created a gulf between themselves as conquerors and the black-brown natives of pre-Aryan India" (Clemens & Blair, 2021; 24).

[22] Darwin had his doubts about the viability of human reason: "the horrid doubt always arises whether the convictions of man's mind, which has been developed from the mind of the lower animals, are of any value

Rather, the Cosmic Order manifests in elect beings — those elected by the will of a beleaguered people — who appear to set aright the attempted subverting of God's eternal will. The Avatāra exists, therefore the vessel does not; that is, the Avatāra is an *event*, not a man — a *state of being*, not a being. This, too, mirrors the Nietzschean vision of the *Übermensch*: it is a collective will, not a man, and certainly no libertine (as so many Shabbos-academicians and Jew-interpreters would have us believe). Both *Übermensch* and Avatāra are reflections of God's will, the collective will of a people oriented to Eternal Nature.

Once we understand the nature of the Paradox, the offense becomes rather obvious: those who cannot bear to live in accordance with the eternal principles of Nature, and certainly cannot bear the appearance of the arbiter of those principles on earth, are immediately and *for all time* offended at the appearance of the Avatāra. Hitler is hated for a reason; we exist in the Kali-Yuga, a time when "most of the population is foolish and not adequately educated," when people are "slow in spiritual realization and always disturbed by various anxieties," when people are "are not serious about self-realization," and when "there is an abundance of strife, ignorance, irreligion and vice."[23] It is *certain* that any appearance of God will be absolutely despised and denounced. Rest assured that, all too often, if the modern world decries it, it is almost certainly good — and so it is with Hitler Avatāra, whose struggle was that of the Good God against the godless golems — *for all time.*

"This was no idle game," the Führer solemnly affirmed before joining Drexler's *Deutsche Arbiter Partei*, "but rather a serious and ardent cause.... Fate itself now seemed to point the way."[24] How could the speaker-vessel see things any other way? This decision, Hitler knew, "would bind me forever, and that there could be no turning back." "The will of eternal Providence" bade him forward. This is precisely why the vessel *does not exist* — there is only the

---

or at all trustworthy" — Darwin Correspondence Project, Letter Number 13230 (1881), http://www.darwinproject.ac.uk/DCP-LETT-13230.

[23] A.C. Bhaktivedanta Swami Prabhupada, *Bhagavad-gītā As It Is* (1972).

[24] *Mein Kampf* vol. 1 (Clemens & Blair, 2017), "The 'German Workers' Party,'" 423.

Avatāra! By becoming the vessel, one ceases to be the vessel. In truth, Hitler had no choice but to fulfill his destiny as Avatāra; he knew it even from an early age, as friend August Kubizek recounts in a childhood experience with the future Führer: "It was as if another being spoke out of [Hitler's] body ... what burst forth from him [was an] elementary force.... It was an unknown youth who spoke to me in that strange hour. He spoke of a special mission which one day would be entrusted to him..."[25] Hitler the man had no choice because God chose *him*; and in that instant, Hitler as historical being ceased to exist — instead, we witness the growing *will of an entire people manifesting the enduring tenets of Nature*. Echoing the words of Krishna Avatāra from ages before, Hitler Avatāra records, *for all time*:

> Nations that make mongrels of their people, or allow their people to be turned into mongrels, sin against the will of eternal Providence. And thus their overthrow at the hands of a stronger opponent cannot be looked upon as wrong but, on the contrary, as a restoration of justice. If a people refuses to guard and uphold the Nature-given qualities that have their roots in the blood, then such a people has no right to complain over the loss of its earthly existence.[26]

Here Providence flatly warns us: *Heed Nature or Nature will not heed you*. It really is as simple as that, and any folk permitting the worst to rise will surely meet their swift demise. It should be noted that "the worst" does not imply "incapable" — "the worst" are those who work against the best interests of blood and folk — albeit quite capably, for the *best* among them would surely be the *worst*. Hitler, too, acknowledged this when he reminds us of the "precondition for every success: Whatever you do, do it thoroughly!"[27] This statement is broadly true, but encourages us to have no misgivings

---

[25] *The Young Hitler I Knew*, "In That Hour It Began..."
[26] *Mein Kampf* vol. 1 (Clemens & Blair, 2017), "Nation and Race," 605.
[27] *Mein Kampf* vol. 2 (Clemens & Blair, 2019), "German Post-War Alliance Policy," 501.

when expunging that which does us harm. All sides of an issue would agree with this, no doubt; but not all sides enjoy the power of quality and Nature reinforcing them.

When one's work is braced by Nature, one's work is *immortal*. This, of course, is why God is immortal. Always reluctant to "speak" or be seen as a writer, Hitler reflected on the difference between the theoretician and the politician:

> While the art of the politician is the art of the possible, the theoretician belongs to those who are said to please the gods, only because they demand the impossible. Such men will always have to renounce present-day fame; but if their ideas are immortal, posterity will grant them its reward.[28]

Hitler was quite fond of the *possible*, quite drawn to immediate action — and immediate action at that.

> Jung refers to Hitler as the prisoner of Wotan, God of storm and hurricane and the Swastika, like some vortex of irresistible energy. Wotan, God of the wind. Therefore the Assault Troops of [Hitlerism] were called *Sturmabteilung*, storm troops, the hurricane. The military campaigns of Hitler all have the same archetype: a hurricane, a storm. He was the creator of *Blitzkrieg*, the lightning war. It could equally be called "Wotan's War."[29]

But equally important was the Führer's concern for posterity, his aspirations for immortality. This was no selfish desire for worldly legacy, for his whole life was an argument against this. One seeking a worldly legacy would have stopped while one was "ahead" — like any selfish politician, so one could write ostentatious memoirs,

---

[28] *Mein Kampf* vol. 1 (Clemens & Blair, 2017), "The Beginning of My Political Activity," 405.

[29] Serrano, *Adolf Hitler: The Ultimate Avatar* (Hermitage Helm, 2014), 173.

build respectable libraries, and get a safe speaking-circuit métier later in life; this is all wholly the opposite of Hitler's impetus. Hitler Avatāra was driven by "a restoration of justice," a cosmic compulsion to uphold the principles underlying all existence; Hitler had no choice — because God made *his*. There was no stopping *der Blitz, der Sturm, der Hurricane*; there is no stopping Wotan. And for this, posterity will grant sure reward.

"I myself have no other aim in the future," Hitler assures us, "than … to devote my whole life, unto my dying breath, to one task: making Germany free, healthy and happy once more."[30] Decisiveness, when trained at the Good, is the path to salvation. The Good is that which transcends and uplifts; it is sacrificing oneself for the benefit of the whole that reflects oneself; this reflection is physical, mental, and spiritual; the Good is *one thing*.[31] Hitler Avatāra was Germany just as Germany was Hitler Avatāra. In Greater Germany's time of need, in the world's time of need — *In order to deliver the pious and to annihilate the miscreants … I advent Myself millennium after millennium* — God appeared, aimed at willing one thing: salvation. *Purity of heart is to will one thing! We know the Paradox exists because we know the Godhead exists; we know the Godhead exists because we see it manifested in history.* "Salvation lies only in the purity with which a man wills the Good."[32] The Good is singular; *willing one thing*, if it is not singular, is, in fact, willing that which is not good — for one is both confused as to the nature of what is willed,[33] and it means we are distanced from God:

> Only the pure in heart can see God, and therefore, draw nigh to Him; and only by God's drawing nigh to them can they maintain this purity. And he who in truth wills only one thing can will only the Good, and

---

[30] 17 August 1934 (speech).
[31] Kierkegaard, *Purity of Heart is to Will One Thing* (Harper, 1956), translated by Douglas Steere, 54: "The Good without condition and without qualification, without preface and without compromise is, absolutely the only thing that a man may and should will, and is only one thing."
[32] Kierkegaard, *Purity* (Harper, 1956), 63.
[33] Kierkegaard, *Purity* (Harper, 1956), 55.

he who only wills only one thing when he wills the
Good can only will the Good in truth.[34]

In devoting his life to a singular task that both *reflected* and *transcended* him, Hitler Avatāra existed as a state of being, he existed as
God; in this way, he won salvation for those pure in heart. Salvation
is the contemplative, decisive pause along the path to the Good; it
is the deep breath of resolution before continuing the steep climb.

"I have surrendered myself to the judgment of the German
folk,"[35] speaks the Führer, and his surrender is, in turn, respite.
"Surrender unto Me; and in return I shall protect you from all sinful
reactions. Therefore, you have nothing to fear."[36] Sin is ostensibly
twofold: (1) multiplicity in one's willing, and (2) actions against
blood and race. Hitler held, "The sin against blood and race is the
original sin in this world. It brings an end to any nation that com-
mits it."[37] Multiplicity in one's willing only derives from the sin
against blood and race; therefore, sin, too, is singular. The Good is
singular: purity of heart — willing one thing — nearness to God —
harmony with Nature. Sin, too, is singular: duplicity of heart —
multiplicity of will and thought — separation from God — disharmony with Nature. In surrendering himself to the judgment of his
people, who both reflected and transcended him, Hitler Avatāra
willed one thing: he represented the Godhead in its mission for the
restoration of eternal principles. Surrendering to the will of that
which reflects and transcends you is not only the restorative breath
before the steep climb, but also harbor from the violent vagaries of
the antagonistic alternative of sin.

∞ ∞ ∞

Adolf Hitler was a particularly soul-stirring speaker; if we say that
his writing was *essential*, we must say that his speaking was *pro-*

---

[34] Kierkegaard, *Purity* (Harper, 1956), 53.
[35] 22 March 1936 (speech).
[36] Bhagavad Gita, XVIII.66.
[37] *Mein Kampf* vol. 1 (Clemens & Blair, 2017), "Causes of the Collapse,"
467.

found. That he hit upon the nerve of *being* — *Dasein* — cannot be debated, for the Avatāra can do no other. Martin Heidegger reminds us of this in his petition to the German people prior to the 12 November 1933 parliamentary election:

> [The future of the German people] is bound to the Führer.... There is only the one will to the full existence [*Dasein*] of the State. The Führer has awakened this will in the entire people and has welded it into a single resolve.[38]

The Avatāra as a *state of being* — *Dasein*; the incarnation of God in a given place and time to restore the will of God and Nature on earth, this battlefield of the Cosmic Struggle; the purity of heart to *will one thing* — the ultimate Good, the reflection and transcendence of the collective will: This is the essence of Hitlerism. Hitler's own words support Heidegger's appeal:

> I do not delude myself that a single person can work miracles on this earth. The miracle lies in the power of a folk itself, given in the plans of God and Nature. *I wish to create this power!* I want to mobilize the best efforts and the highest values of this folk so that this folk will stand firm on its own and thus *make me strong again. The power of this folk is my power, and its strength is my strength!*[39]

Hitler Avatāra here speaks of creation through reciprocation, which is the essence of the Divine's incarnation and mission: Reveal the latent power of God in the folk; with the revelation comes creative release — the expression of the collective *will-to-power*, which is to say, the *Übermensch.* God creates power by tapping into the unconscious recesses of a people submerged under the spans of time.

---

[38] *Freiburger Studentenzeitung,* "German Men and Women," 10 November 1933, translated by William Lewis.
[39] 27 March 1936 (speech); emphasis added.

What is discovered? — That which is transcended is reflected in the transcendent: *God helps those who help themselves!* When God revealed itself to Arjuna, the man was awed: "Your form ... is fiery and immeasurable like the sun" and "You are the supreme primal objective ... [and] the maintainer of religion, the eternal Personality of God" who stands as "refuge of the universe"![40] *Das Hakenkreuz* is the sign of the sun, chosen by Hitler to represent the *primal objective* of the Aryan folk reestablishing their divine roots, of elevating the primacy of blood and soil in the spirit of the Germanic folk, which will provide refuge *for all time.* They have only to rekindle the "fire that, in the form of knowledge, illuminated the dark night by drawing aside the veil of mystery, showing man how to rise up and become master over all the other earthly beings"[41] — the infinite form of the Führer is this fire, sparked by the paradoxical revelation of the finite human spirit. From this revelation, the Avatāra avows, "I again create."[42]

The creative power of the Führer was conferred to him by the very people who needed their power rekindled. "For who am I?" asks Hitler, "I am nothing other than your speaker, German folk, the speaker for your rights! You have vested your trust in me! I will prove myself worthy of this trust."[43] The symbiosis of folk, Reich, and Führer was the source of collective and individual pride and gratitude: "I myself am infinitely proud to be allowed to be the Führer of this folk, and I am grateful to the Lord for every hour which He gives me to contribute."[44] *God helps those who help themselves!* Yet, at the same time, God appears as Avatāra when man needs him most. Thus the mystery is revealed.

∞ ∞ ∞

Hitler indeed was and is *the* speaker, and here we read his words; we are also fortunate enough to have record of his voice — so that

---

[40] Bhagavad Gita XI.17-18, 37.
[41] *Mein Kampf* vol. 1 (Clemens & Blair, 2017), "Nation and Race," 537.
[42] Bhagavad Gita XI.7.
[43] 30 January 1940 (speech).
[44] 10 September 1943 (speech).

we might witness God as he, in part, manifested less than a century ago. We see how Hitler the man was really Hitler Avatāra; we sense the divine words and see, *quite clearly*, that God and Nature never change — whether we study the Bhagavad Gita or *Mein Kampf*, divinity endures. Any true Avatāra would attest to and embody the eternal being of God, of Nature, and speak of divine paramountcy in a world full of miscreants; and, naturally, any true Avatāra would be condemned because of this.

Hitler saw himself as a speaker, but also a recorder — for past and posterity. He substantiated the Paradox, which can only be reviled in this most faithless and darkest age. As with all avatars, Hitler brought the message most pressing for his time and place: the Myth of the Blood, that *Blut und Boden* are the spiritual-cultural (i.e., *racial*) foundation of all life. This foundation, once upheld by the spiritual-aristocracy, was ultimately abandoned for material gain; thus the once-dignified Aryan elite became mere instruments of internationalist Jews — Jews who want nothing more than to drive an eternal wedge between Nature's racial harmony and the folks of this world meant to sustain it. *For all time*, Hitler Avatāra revealed man's greatest danger: the satanic, degenerative disharmony propagated by the demiurgical Jew.

Now, with an understanding of how the Führer saw himself, we are prepared to investigate the Paradox — of man, of God.

— 3 —
Hitler Paradoxa

Adolf Hitler was an absolute genius. He was years ahead of all his followers. No one could come near him or understand him.

— Arno Breker

When generations of inculcated insouciance confront the Paradox, the air alights with ember. A herald from the vacuum meets the friction of atmosphere and illuminates the sky, if only for a moment; *it is the forerunner of a new time.* In its wake comes that which sets the earth ablaze. *For whom should we fight now, my Führer?* Now we fight for the MAN TO COME.

1945 — a sign of things to come: *Götterdämmerung.* Where one finds victory, another sees defeat. An overarching urge shapes one's view: *tamas, rajas, sattva* — the *gunas* upon which *varna* was based. The former, *tamas* — listless ignorance — governs most, hence the prevailing view that catastrophe was and is the sensible course in the face of Hitlerist *nonconformity* — that is, *light-bringing enlightenment* — in a dark world. The *tamasic* accept the conformist view as docilely as they do the authority of those spewing it: the *tamasic* happily swap freedom for security simply because they were never free to begin with: they were born into bondage and will never escape:

> Under this category [which consists of the majority of people] fall all those who haven't been born to think for themselves or who haven't learned to do so, and who — partly through incompetence and partly through ignorance — believe everything they read. This group includes that type of lazy individual who, although capable of thinking for himself, absorbs what others have thought, assuming that they must have

put some effort into it. The influence of the press on all these people is therefore enormous; they are, after all, the broad masses of a nation. They aren't willing or able to personally sift through what is being served up to them, and so their whole attitude towards daily problems is almost solely the result of outside influence. All this ... is catastrophic when done at the hand of scoundrels and liars.[1]

Scoundrels and *liars* work incessantly to shape public opinion, and they, in turn, represent their master, the Lord of Darkness. *Tamas* is more than ignorance: it is darkness. *Darkness, lethargy, ignorance, wickedness* — these are all synonymous, all complementary. The masses are *tamasic*; their ignorance and incompetence make them *wicked*, particularly when whipped into frenzy by those more capable; in this case, the more capable are passionate (*rajasic*), but not good (*sattvic*).[2] The passionate who work for the forces of darkness are the *scoundrels* and *liars*, for they set the will of the masses against the light, the good. Again, *the Good is that which transcends and uplifts; it is sacrificing oneself for the benefit of the whole that reflects oneself; this reflection is physical, mental, and spiritual; the Good is one thing.* The Good is the blood in your veins that both does and does not belong to you: the Myth of the Blood. Hitler unmasked the Jews as the *scoundrels* and *liars* inciting the masses against the light God brings to this demiurgical world; Jews are behind every kind of demonic act meant to undermine and usurp Nature's enlightening harmony; *they cannot do otherwise*; Jews are the (anti-)race *par excellence*.

Nietzsche said, "The devil has the most extensive perspectives for God; on that account he keeps so far away from him: — the devil, in effect, as the oldest friend of knowledge."[3] For Nietzsche, "God" is the Judeo-Christian Jehovah — the Jewish god of *darkness*,

---

[1] *Mein Kampf* vol. 1 (Clemens & Blair, 2017), "Causes of the Collapse," 455.
[2] We might think of the *gunas*, which undergird all material existence, as a spectrum: *bad – passion – good :: tamas – rajas – sattva*. *Rajas* is neither good nor bad, but can be used for either *tamasic* or *sattvic* purposes.
[3] *Beyond Good and Evil*, ch. 4 §129, translated by Helen Zimmern.

of *ignorance*. Jehovah desires and agitates for mass ignorance because the vacant torpidity it spawns manufactures "victory." Conversely, the "devil" is Jehovah's counterpoint — the "devil" is the *Lichtbringer*, Lucifer, the "oldest friend of knowledge."[4] The scoundrels' and liars' ploy: demonize that which is good and the battle is half over. Hence the light-bringer is the "devil" to the Judeo-Christian "god." And that which was up is down, that which was good is bad, that which was light is dark. Hence victory is defeat; 1945 — the harbinger of things to come. But even more than this: *incipit Judeus* — the beginning of the end, the acceleration of the Kali-Yuga.

Defeat is also victory, however. *Götterdämmerung* brought us closer to the Jews' desired end: Jewish supremacy over an enslaved hive fetishizing liberty, equality, and other abstract fabrications meant to slander Aryan distinctiveness and undermine the natural order. Nature's foundations — *race, biological sex, inequality, fitness* — these become mere "social constructs" or mountains to be leveled: cosmic dissemblance to confuse and compel the indolent masses ripe for the hiving.[5] *Rajasic* cadres stir their commissar-

---

[4] For more on the difference between Satan (Jehovah) and Lucifer (Wotan, the Aryan God), see *Myth and Sun: Essays of the ARCHETYPE* (Clemens & Blair, 2022). That "Satan" and "Lucifer" have been conflated is naught but Jewish trickery meant to keep the unwitting forever in the dark — an apt deception from the Lord of Darkness, Demiurge-Jehovah.

[5] Examples of Judeo-Liberalistic subversion: "The United Nations Educational, Scientific, and Cultural Organization (UNESCO) drafted its statement on the 'race question' in 1950 [which was meant to bury "Nazi" science and propagate the notion that race is a "social construct"].... Its authors were: Morris Ginsberg, a Jewish sociologist interested in the 'liberal disposition'; Claude Lévi-Strauss, a Jewish anthropologist whose structural anthropology is founded on the premise that all cultures are essentially equal; Ashley Montagu, a Jewish anthropologist who zealously called race 'man's most dangerous myth'; Juan Comas, a Spanish communist and anthropologist; Humayun Kabir, an Indian politician who served in the administrations of communist prime ministers; Luis de Aguiar Costa Pinto, a Brazilian sociologist aligned with the communist Brazilian Workers' Party; Ernest Beaglehole, a New Zealander psychologist whose brother and confidant, John Beaglehole, was influenced by the Jewish communist Harold Laski; and E. Franklin Frazier, a black sociologist who rose to prominence writing of the 'black proletari-

cauldrons, enflaming the mob into delirium, ready to uncondition-ally accept and vehemently defend their role in the hive. This Jewish victory goes by other names: *Liberalism, capitalism, humanism, international socialism, scientism, Marxism, globalism, positivism, psychoanalysis* [disassembling the *psyche,* or *soul*], *consumerism, materialism, communism, deconstructionism, atheism.* All of these practices have but one meaning: *Jewish supremacy,* or the disman-tling of Nature and the subjugation of Aryan lifeways. Yet when "the [Jew] thinks he has achieved victory, we quickly find just the opposite happens: *the danger becomes ever greater.* He begins to fear for the end of his illusory existence."[6] The danger does indeed

---

at' and under the intellectual aegis of the Jew Isaac Rice. Despite such allegiances and, in fact, how their statement itself reads, we must *believe* the authors' motivations are entirely *objective.* This, of course, is akin to believing the sheep would be unbiased in its assessment of the wolf" (from *Myth and Sun: Essays of the ARCHETYPE,* 228). The "gender" fabrica-tion has even more seedy origins, being the brainchild of Weimar Jews (Magnus Hirschfeld, Ludwig Levy-Lenz, and Felix Abraham) and John Money. The former enabled the mentally ill in quests for social-sexual deviance; the latter used his profession to abuse children, much like his predecessor, Alfred Kinsey. We are told these satanic degenerates are "pioneering" and "influential" — indeed, in a world full of miscreants, they certainly are. The Civil Rights Movement in America, which codi-fied the absurd notion of mass equality, itself disproved daily by reality, overlapped with the terroristic Cultural Revolution in Communist China — *mere coincidence,* no doubt. Finally, fitness itself is even disparaged: mental fitness is undermined by Jewish psychotherapeutic and pharma-ceutical prescriptions; physical fitness is undermined by Judeo-capitalist food profiteering, wherein *quantity* supplants *quality* and cheap, pro-cessed ingredients become the norm, which, in turn, deteriorate physical health and undermine mental fitness; moreover, any adherence to strict healthy living and traditionalist values is deemed "right-wing" and "ex-tremist" (e.g., "The White Supremacist Origins of Exercise," Time [2022], and "Granola Nazis: Digital Traditionalism, the Folkish Movement and the Normalization of the Far-Right," GNET [2023]); spiritual fitness is therefore precluded without mental and physical fitness; too, spiritual fitness is essentially seen as anachronistic in this age of Scientific (Liber-alistic) faith.

[6] Miguel Serrano, *Manu: For the Man to Come* (Hermitage Helm, 2017), 177.

become greater, for the Jew will press even more obsessively to sustain the unsustainable: the Organic Lie *cannot do otherwise*. This is the acceleration of time that precedes life's governed apocalypse.[7]

> Everything these *Golem* [the Jews and their helpers] attempt ... will not have the desired effect, even going so far as to use hypnotic influences on the masses will fail.... Jehovah and his *Golem* will annihilate each other within their automatized Universe, together with the society of ants they foster. That will be the end of *Kali-Yuga*.[8]

Thus their victory secures their ruin, and one side of the cosmic event is revealed: the paradoxical herald from the vacuum burns up in the rajasic-tamasic resistance. But that which has won is undone, and another side awaits revelation.

Victory in defeat: this is the mantra of the *Minnesinger*, the love of the gods. Karna, whose tale is recorded in the Mahabharata, is an exemplar of this mantra. Born unto the sun god, Surya, Karna was nonetheless abandoned by his young mother, Kunti, for being born out of wedlock. He was found and raised by a Sudra family of charioteers. Despite this, Karna's blood belied his lowly status and he felt the highborn pull of his divine lineage: he would be a warrior, a seeker of honor and glory. He first sought Drona, master teacher of martial arts, who rejected him for his Sudra background; then he disguised himself as a Brahman and approached Parashurama, quickly becoming the great teacher's best student. Karna's skill was renowned and rivaled only by Arjuna's (his still unknown brother). At a skills competition, Arjuna was the favored competitor, but Karna bested him in every way, earning the crowd's adoration. Karna's lowly status was revealed, however, and Arjuna's family, the Pandavas, questioned the legitimacy of Karna's victory since Sudras were not eligible to participate in the contest. One man, Duryodhana, came to Karna's defense, despite his Sudra status and because of his unparalleled skill; Karna was deeply moved by

---

[7] *Myth and Sun: Essays of the ARCHETYPE* (Clemens & Blair, 2022).
[8] Serrano, *Manu* (Hermitage Helm, 2017), 184.

Duryodhana's act and would remain loyal to him unto death — this, despite Krishna promising him a kingdom and restored honor amongst the revered Pandavas.

This loyalty is key to everything: *Meine Ehre heißt Treue — My honor is loyalty.* Karna's loyalty trumped even Krishna's plea, for loyalty itself *is* divine. Karna was true to his blood, which compelled him to strive for more than what "social constructs" dictated; Karna was true to Duryodhana, who defended his honor when the world seemed to stand against him; Karna was true to honor itself — because his *honor is loyalty* — because his honor spoke from his soul and drove him upwards despite all appearances. Karna was born of the sun, Surya, Apollo, *der Lichtbringer*, Lucifer — he brought the light of loyalty to this darkened world bereft of honor. The Swastika is the sign of the sun. Karna represents the Holy Swastika, whose honor is loyalty — the Holy Swastika, which represents Aryan lifeways: defenders of blood and family, respectful of Nature, upholders of faith and fitness.

Because of his loyalty to Duryodhana, Karna was pit against Arjuna in the great Kurukshetra War. The Son of the Sun was the light "destroying the darkness" as he turned the tide of war to his side's favor, "slaying large numbers ... along his way."[9] Arjuna, however, was up to the task, balancing the sides through his inspired effort. Karna was defiant nonetheless: *If Death himself were to protect Arjuna in battle, I would yet stand and fight him; I will kill him or die a hero's death!*[10] The "hero's death" is assured because honor is loyalty and loyalty is honor. When at last the rivals met on the battlefield, Karna's chariot became mired in the earth. "It's against the rules of war to attack an unarmed man with his back turned," Karna reminded Arjuna. Setting down his bow and alighting his chariot, Karna turned to dislodge the wheel; seeing Karna unarmed and disengaged, Arjuna hesitated, knowing his half-brother was right; Krishna nevertheless urged Arjuna to take the opportunity and kill the great warrior, for God knew the war would only end if Karna,

---

9 Mahabharata, Karna Parva, §37, §56, all translations by Kisari Ganguli unless otherwise noted.
10 Mahabharata, Karna Parva, §37.

born of the sun and loyal unto death, ceased to be. Arjuna took the shot, severing Karna's head, wetting the earth with loyalty's blood.

> Karna's severed head looked beautiful — like a mountain summit unclouded by a tempest, or a quenched fire after the sacrifice, or the image of the sun after it has reached the hills. The Karna-sun, with arrows for its rays, after having scorched the hostile army, was at last set by the mighty Arjuna.... Desirous of beholding the heroic Karna, ... stretched on the earth like the sun dropped from the skies, the field's warriors stood in awe around the fallen hero.... Upon the fall of Karna, the sky became enveloped in darkness; the earth trembled; meteors tore through the sky and dazzled the eye.... Hail Karna, who was worshipped by the gods...[11]

More than luck ended Karna[12] — it was divine will. Why did Krishna help Arjuna kill Karna? Presumably, it was because Karna was involved in the humiliation of Draupadi, wife of the five Pandava brothers. And, Karna indeed acted shamefully, calling Draupadi *whorish* and demanding that she be disrobed before the court after one of her husbands lost her in a dice game; it was only Krishna that came to her aid, preventing her disrobement. Karna's behavior, though, was precipitated by Draupadi's public humiliation of him, as she refused him participation in a skills competition because of his lowborn status (as charioteer). This was the second time the Pandavas publicly humiliated Karna, so his actions were, in his mind, retribution for ignominious Pandavan behavior. One disgraceful act does not warrant another, but the motivations for Karna's conduct become clearer. Yet this is not why Krishna willed Karna's death.

Krishna, by killing him, made a hero of Karna. Karna ceaselessly, and seemingly, faced a world full of enemies; and despite this, he

---

[11] Mahabharata, Karna Parva, §91, §92, §94, translation modified for readability.

[12] Mahabharata, Karna Parva, §91.

never faltered. Karna was the son of a god and a princess, but the fates decreed he would be raised a Sudra, the lowest caste. He felt a spiritual-cultural pull toward something higher; *the memory of the blood* drove him upward. Against all odds he became a warrior, the prize pupil of a renowned teacher and rivaled only by the gifted Arjuna; he became a powerful speaker, which raised him to a "point of dignity and intrinsic nobility"[13]; he was appointed king and military commander, leader of the valiant doomed; and, perhaps most strikingly, he was a loyal friend — even unto death. Deeply spurned by his public belittlements, loyalty meant something *more* to Karna. If the divine is that which is perpetually and tantalizingly out of reach, then loyalty was surely sublime to jilted Karna. When Duryodhana defended the warrior's honor, Karna was moved to a point of unshakeable devotion; he had never experienced it before: someone staying true to him, someone acknowledging his clear and natural ability. In this, Karna represented that which even Krishna could not resist: the Paradox.

The Son of the Sun and his heroic loyalty could not be fully realized unless the source was slain. Thus it was that victory was secured in death. In this, Krishna fulfilled the promise of Karna, the divine and paradoxical promise: the promise of loyalty unto death — *the assurance of things hoped for, the conviction of things unseen.* Krishna pushed Arjuna, not to kill Karna, but to midwife faith.

> I believe and declare that a folk should value nothing more highly than the dignity and freedom of its existence — that it must defend these to the last drop of blood.

> That it has no holier duty to fulfill, no higher law to obey.

> That the shame of a cowardly submission can never be erased.

---

[13] Kevin McGrath, *The Sanskrit Hero: Karṇa in Epic Mahābhārata* (Brill, 2004), 176, 144.

> That this drop of poison in the blood of a folk is passed
> on to its descendants and will corrupt and undermine
> the strength of future generations....

> That a folk bravely fighting for its freedom is invincible.

> That even the loss of freedom after an honorable and
> bloody battle secures the rebirth of the folk and is the
> seed of life from which, one day, a new tree will strike
> firm root....[14]

With these words, Carl von Clausewitz, a great influence for Hitler, describes *faith* — not a faith of the meek, but that of the strong and noble.[15] *I believe, future, invincible, never, must, one day* — this is assurance of things hoped for, conviction of things unseen. Coupled with Clausewitz's anticipation are words of struggle: *last drop of blood, no holier duty, no higher law, bravely fighting, bloody battle, strike firm root*, and so on. Faith and struggle, then, are at the heart of Clausewitz's *Political Testament*. Likewise, faith and struggle underpinned all of Hitler's actions; he spoke time and again of absolute and unshakeable faith as the foundation of the Movement: "This Movement is committed to the task of restoring loyalty, faith and decency..." and "Faith is everything [we] have in this world!"[16] *Loyalty, faith,* and *decency* encapsulate God: all Avatāra manifest to restore bygone purity.

This is done through example: Karna exemplified divine will by dying because of it. The faith of the fallen is superior to any material success of the heedless precisely because of the meaning impregnating the faithful life. "Let him beware who has no faith," cautioned the Führer, for "he is committing a sin against the meaning

---

[14] From his *Political Testament* (1812).

[15] Hitler echoed Clausewitz in a 08 November 1934 speech, "Only cowards abandon their own cause, and that continues to take effect and spread like an insidious drop of poison. And then the realization dawns that it is still better, if necessary, to accept a horrible but sudden end than to bear horrors without end."

[16] From 14 October 1933 and 01 May 1935 speeches, respectively.

of life as a whole."[17] Adolf Hitler's fight, like that of Krishna and Karna, was restorative; theirs was a combat against the *heedless*, the *godless*, the *faithless* hordes of modernity who fail to see meaning even in their own relentless persecution of those who cannot but believe. The Avatāra exists because these Nihilists aim to undo all that is good, all that uplifts. Nihilism is the secular ritual of those who hate; it is the language of modernity, the language of the "victors" — the liberal-democratic-international socialistic-globalist world; it is, as Nietzsche said, "the absolute repudiation of worth" wherein "the inferior [mass of society] inflates its needs into cosmic and metaphysical values ... [and] tyrannizes over the [exceptional few], so that these lose their belief in themselves and [in turn] become Nihilists";[18] it is therefore the eternal enemy of God and all those who seek the divine Good.

Faith is Nihilism's antipode: Hitler fought to restore faith: This is why Adolf Hitler is hated. Hitler Avatāra extracted the Sisyphean myth from the Nihilist's grasp: no longer is Sisyphus woefully and futilely pushing a stone up a hill of despair; instead, he is an *Übermensch*: he *wills* his burden despite his destiny. He is fated to eternally force the stone up a mountain, and yet he pushes; yet he wills. In this way, the stone becomes *his* stone; the mountain becomes *his* mountain. Through the power of his will, the frenzied externals are tamed. As the faithful man wills, he lives.

"From the sacrifice of our soldiers and my own solidarity with them unto death, a seed will one day germinate in German history [bringing] about the shining rebirth of the National Socialist movement and the realization of a true *Volksgemeinschaft*."[19] Hitler speaks here of Clausewitz's "rebirth of the folk" and "the seed of life from which, one day, a new tree will strike firm root." It is *Götterdämmerung* which creates the conditions for enduring change, and real, spiritual victory can only come from individual, material death. Karna died so something greater — *epochal inspiration* — might live. Krishna goaded Arjuna's arrow to stress Karna's faith

---

[17] 14 September 1936 (speech).
[18] *The Will to Power* (B&N, 2006), translated by Anthony Ludovici, Book I §3, §27.
[19] Adolf Hitler, "My Political Testament," 29 April 1945.

and loyalty — for faith and loyalty surpass even the ostensibly righteous. Karna knew that when he alighted the chariot, his life was over — *and yet he alighted!* In this way, Karna exemplified loyalty to his cosmic duty; his duty was not to die, but to be faithful and loyal to the end, for this is what those in his life routinely lacked; he would thus now be the inspiration for all those *faithful* and *loyal*, and in this way, would embody what it means to *love*.

Pandavas, Kauravas — brothers fighting brothers in the Kurukshetra War of the Mahabharata; one's side matters not; what matters are the cosmic principles upheld or discarded for the sake of one's spiritual-cultural milieu. When one struggles for faith, loyalty, and duty, one lives within the Supreme God. *What is done out of love always takes place beyond good and evil!*[20] Hitler, too, was the vessel through which God spoke; he prophesied the resurgence of that which was sacrificed for the life of those who died, the life of those who have not yet come; and by *becoming* the vessel, he *ceased to be* the vessel: his was the message of transcendent Providence: *Faith is existential*: One frees oneself by yielding to the transcendent. *I have taught you to have faith, now give me your faith!* Thus spoke the Führer, Hitler Avatāra.[21]

Hitler won the war by losing it. Like Karna, "He triumphed because he had conquered *Himself*, the temptation to victory in an untimely moment not chosen by Him, but by the Enemy. He won ... within *Himself*..."[22] When one ceases to be the vessel precisely because one is the vessel, what occurs is transcendence through faith — though it is not the faith of the individual acting which ignites transcendence, but the faith of those inspired by the act. Time itself is transcended because the Avatāra is an *event*, not a man — a *state of being*, not a being: the faith of those to come creates both past and present. Thus Clausewitz's *rebirth* is yet the *birth*; thus Hitler's *seed* is yet the *tree*; thus Karna's *alighting* is yet the *ascending*. *Götterdämmerung* is the unstated middle: we create the conditions for resurgence by our faith in it. We — the *faithful* — are em-

---

[20] Nietzsche, *Beyond Good and Evil*, ch. 4 §153.
[21] 20 March 1936 (speech).
[22] Serrano, *Manu* (Hermitage Helm, 2017), 42; emphasis added.

powered and uplifted by our faith in that which is beyond materiality. Both the act of the Godhead and our equally essential faith in it
secure real, spiritual victory — the only victory that means anything because it births both past and future — for "we who were
very young, and even for the yet unborn who now have come to
reincarnate and fight as born Hitlerists without knowing themselves why."[23] We fight because it is in our blood — *the memory of
the blood*. We have been a part of this Cosmic Struggle since the
beginning; it is our entire purpose for being here. Hitler Avatāra
made our existence possible, and we created him. Hitlerism makes
possible the final victory — the only victory with any meaning; that
it exists assures its triumph, for it has already happened.

∞ ∞ ∞

The Germanic tends to a dark vision of the world — but a vision
free of moral and spiritual corruption, and one rather obscuring a
most profound trait: loyalty. *Loyalty at all costs*. The darkness
stems from a remote separation from God, offering in return its toll
of incisive discernment: we see the Lord of Darkness ceaselessly
striving to stifle us for all time. Our salvation is the Golden Thread
of loyalty, warming the cold abyss, softening the barbed edges,
lighting the emergent Aryan soul. Come what may, if we have any
Aryan pneuma left, we remain loyal to our ancestors and fighters
for our descendants — anything less than this is the blackened
canvas of slavery. This *light of loyalty*, this *fire of faith* is the chiaroscuro of Rembrandt, the most individualistic of the individualistic,
freedom-loving Germans.[24]

> "To have character and to be German is the same
> thing," says Fichte... [The Germanic] tendency to indi-
> vidualism, which resulted in the familiar German dis-
> unity that has so often been politically detrimental,

---

[23] Serrano, *Manu* (Hermitage Helm, 2017), 169.
[24] Julius Langbehn, *Rembrandt as Educator* (1890), "German Character"
and "Chiaroscuro."

enables him especially to achieve more in the artistic-
intellectual field than other folk. *Individuality* is the
root of all art, and since the Germans are undoubtedly
the most original, idiosyncratic, and individualistic of
all peoples, they are also — if they succeed in reflecting
the world clearly — the artistically most significant of
all peoples.[25]

And so we witness the enlivening light: it salvages the dark project
of Demiurge-Jehovah with the miracle of triumphant will: "The only thing that counts is man and his creative work."[26] From creativity
comes freedom, and we can only create when we mirror God: in
faith, loyalty, and adherence to divine Nature — the mirror then
reflects our own self. Hitler Avatāra reversed the mechanizing pull
of time through his struggle for Aryan freedom: he reinstated faith
in this gutter-world of golems, despite their war against him, despite their material victory and continued push for the digitized
hive of mankind, which will turn every colluder into food for an
insatiable Satan. Hitler Avatāra unmasked the Eternal Enemy, "the
most evil enemy of the world of all time"[27] — *for all time* — and
thus restored freedom to a freedom-loving folk.

There has never been an un-free Aryan — not on trial, not in
prison, not even in death. For the Aryan is twice born: born into the
demiurgical darkness of a world intent on his ruin, and born into
the divine light of another world, a creative source, a parallel *Paradesha* where eternal victory has already been won.[28] The subject

---

[25] Langbehn, *Rembrandt as Educator*, "German Individualism."
[26] Serrano, *Manu* (Hermitage Helm, 2017), 194.
[27] Adolf Hitler, 30 January 1942 (speech). And from the Führer's "Political
Testament" (29 April 1945): "Centuries will go by, but from the ruins of
our cities and monuments of art, hatred for the people who are ultimately responsible will always renew itself; against those whom we have to
thank for all this: international Jewry and its helpers!"
[28] *Paradesha*, that is, the "High Polar Region," also called *Aryavarsha* —
the land of the enlightened *Arya* beyond Boreas, the Arctic home of the
Vedas, the land of the white, radiant spirits faithful to the Sun, whose
sign is the Swastika. "Those who intend to someday return to Paradesha

of chiaroscuro — the twice born — channels the light revealing him and projects it back on the source, feeding the reflection. And so the paradox reveals the Paradox.

∞ ∞ ∞

The Paradox lives in the truth that if the vessel exists, faith cannot. No movement, if it ever amounted to anything, exists without faith. Hitlerism exists because Hitler the man did not. Moreover, Hitlerism can only exist in the future if Hitler the man did not. The present work is dedicated to the tenet that Hitler Avatāra was God, not a vessel; once the vessel existed, it ceased existing and God was revealed; furthermore, the revelation of God is the spiritual-cultural unity of a folk; Adolf Hitler was the embodiment of this unity, the concentration of a collective will. The only possibility of Hitlerism enduring is if it becomes a matter of faith; the only possibility of Nature enduring is if the Aryan folk recognize the validity of Hitlerism. There is thus Hitlerism — or all is finished.

Adolf Hitler is seen in myriad ways: by detractors as *evil, belligerent, indiscriminate,* and a *madman* — by supporters as *bold, peaceable, fundamentally good,* and an *exemplary leader.* Despite appearances to the contrary, the two sides are actually joined in their lack of faith — thus, they are essentially equal in their progress toward a world-catastrophe from which there is no redemption. The detractors are entrenched in their position, so one cannot expect their course to change. The supporters, however, must go beyond mere temporal successes and measurable indices as the lens from which to view the Führer; that is, an understanding of *Hitler the man* or *Hitler the world-historical person* must be cast aside.

In his assessment of Christianity, Kierkegaard noted that "Christendom has done away with Christianity, without being quite aware of it. The consequence is that, if anything is to be done, one

---

must do so with the Leftwards Swastika, rotating backwards towards the polar origin" (Serrano, *Manu,* 77).

must try again to introduce Christianity to Christendom."[29] The same can be said of Hitlerism: the modern — or, rather, Judeo-materialist — view that all things must be "analytically understood" has seeped into former domains of faith. Christendom expelled Christianity because "the vain chatter of history" turned Christ "fantastically into something other than He is..."[30] Christ became mere man, a specimen in the laboratory of world history — a figure to be examined, understood, and contextualized; what this leaves, however, is a faithless doctrine that lends itself to globalist machinations — the "believer" simply takes solace in the Beatitudes, attends occasional mass, and continues to put his socks on, one foot at a time, for the continuation of a world order that aims to enslave him. *Believing*, in fact, plays no part in this charade. Instead, the "believer" has, quite simply, an *understanding* of Christ's divinity in much the same way he has an understanding of the previous day's box scores: all's well that ends well, and 2,000 years of certitude over Christ's status is as certain as any morning report. But rest assured: "About [Christ] nothing can be known; He can only be believed."[31]

Hitler's supporters and sympathizers likewise detract from final, faithful victory when all they see are the regenerative infrastructure projects, revitalizing social programs, skillful statecraft, and military wonders of the Reich. These are but proofs — "proofs [that] might serve to make a man attentive, so that once he has become attentive he may arrive at the point of deciding whether he will believe or be offended."[32] For Kierkegaard and Christianity, the "offense" lies in (1) a man declaring he is God and (2) Christ's lowly status. A contemporary of Christ could *only* be offended at these things; faith comes despite the offense — and because of it. Today, one is not "offended" by the remarkable material achievements within Hitler's Reich, but the spiritual-cultural restoration meant to reorient a folk to Nature, to its natural roots.

Part of this folk-restoration is the eradication of those elements harmful to its continued existence: *To deliver the pious and*

---

29 Kierkegaard, *Training in Christianity* (Vintage, 2004), 31.
30 Kierkegaard, *Training in Christianity* (Vintage, 2004), 33.
31 Kierkegaard, *Training in Christianity* (Vintage, 2004), 20.
32 Kierkegaard, *Training in Christianity* (Vintage, 2004), 83.

to annihilate the miscreants ... I advent Myself millennium after mil-lennium.[33] One is therefore "offended" at the treatment of the miscreants in Hitler's Reich; of course, because the miscreants control the mass of money and information, and are increasingly brazen in their assumption of governmental positions, they are no longer *miscreants* but *hapless victims*. And because of their control over such materiality, they thus control the *tamasic* and willing-*rajasic* masses that are now ready to do their bidding.

We are left, then, with two kinds of Hitler-sympathizers: (1) the one who says, "He did good things, but..." and (2) the one who says, "Some things were necessary and had their place, but now is a different time and we must move on..." In the former case, indoctrination has had its effect; frankly, it's a real wonder this person even acknowledges the positives of that era, as all of Judeo-history is aimed at rewriting the past to accommodate a grossly Jewish present. This "He did good things, but..." is the refrain of one who has an inkling that *something* of what's been taught is amiss, but is largely unsure of how to proceed in challenging long-held, approved narratives. Whether or not this person moves beyond this stage is dependent upon his personality — *is the initial curiosity sufficient to catalyze further inquiry?* — and upon his fortuitous encounters with countervailing revisions to Judeo-history. The latter case is more inimical than the former: The "we must move on" type has it all figured out — there is no moving him; he pays lip service to traditionalist causes, but does not and will not see that blood sits as their foundation; he is therefore, essentially, a rightist Christian: traditionalist on the outside, leftist on the inside. Both the former and the latter are susceptible to the miscreants' media.

> And in the primitive simplicity of their minds, they
> more readily fall victims to the Big Lie than the small
> lie, since they themselves often tell small lies in little
> matters, but would be ashamed to resort to large-scale
> falsehoods. It would never occur to them to fabricate
> colossal untruths, and they would not believe that oth-

---

[33] Bhagavad Gita IV.8.

ers could have the impudence to distort the truth so infamously.

Even though the facts that prove this are clear, they will still doubt and waver, and will continue to think that there must be some other explanation. The grossly impudent lie always leaves traces behind it, even after it has stuck — a fact that is known to all artful liars in this world, and to all who conspire together in the art of lying. These people know only too well how to use falsehood for the basest of purposes.

From time immemorial, however, the Jews have known better than any others how to exploit falsehood and calumny. Their very existence is based on one great lie, namely, that they are a religious community and not a race. And what a race. One of the greatest thinkers of mankind has branded them for all time with a statement that is profoundly and precisely true: he called them "The great master of the lie." Those who don't realize the truth of that statement, or don't wish to believe it, will never be able to lend a hand in this world to help truth prevail.[34]

This often-misquoted passage from Hitler's *Mein Kampf* applies not only to the *tamasic* and willing-*rajasic* masses, but also to the abovementioned hostile "sympathizers." In any case, the Jews have swayed them; and because continued cooperation with (or, at least, non-hostility toward) the prevailing world order is incentivized, such "sympathizers" will likely never take the next step and shrug off the Jewish yoke of coerced compliance: for them, faith means nothing; they are captive to Judeo-*understanding*.

Faith is an individual choice: it is freedom, *for all time*, for the individual. This freedom "gives existence elasticity" and changes "the corruptible into the incorruptible." *It is for freedom, therefore,*

---

[34] Adolf Hitler, *Mein Kampf* vol. 1 (Clemens & Blair, 2017), "Causes of the Collapse," 439, 441; Hitler quotes Schopenhauer.

that I am fighting — for the time to come...[35] When one is confronted with the dilemma of accepting either individual suffering ("everything must have an end") or boundless finitude ("nothing has an
end," or, "the individual's negative absorption in existence"), it is
freedom that comes to the rescue: faith releases us from universali-
ty's Nihilistic grasp and forges in us the will to create a destiny that
stands defiantly in the face of an ethical order meant to erase us.[36]
The freedom of faith gives everything a heroic end, for it enables us
to transcend the universal and suspend the ethical. Kierkegaard
talks of the "leap" — this "inner deed [that] is the true life of freedom."[37] One must make the leap *away from* understanding; one
must leap *to* something unknown. For this reason, the faithful person cannot and should not try to *convince* anyone, for *convincing*
lies outside the realm of faith. — *What our generation lacks is not
reflection but passion.*[38] — Rather, one can only offer the "proofs
[that] might serve to make a man attentive, so that once he has become attentive he may arrive at the point of *deciding* whether he
will believe or be offended."[39] If he believes and swaps understanding for passion, a victory in this Cosmic Struggle has been won; if
he remains offended, then he was lost from the start and his service
to the cause would have never been fruitful — consider this, therefore, a victory *nonetheless*.

It is important to recapitulate here the significance of the "offense." One takes offense at that which the understanding cannot
understand: *How can Adolf Hitler, a man who did many wondrous
and terrible things, be God? He was, after all, just a man — and one
with a bohemian nature at that!* This is presumably the gist of the
hostile's thought. Yet we know that "To deliver the pious and to

---

[35] Kierkegaard, *Either/Or*, Part II, "Development of the Personality" (II
141) (Princeton UP, 1987), translated by H. and E. Hong.
[36] Kierkegaard, *Either/Or*, Part II, "Postscriptum."
[37] Kierkegaard, *Either/Or*, Part II, "Development of the Personality" (II
141).
[38] Kierkegaard, *Fear and Trembling* (Princeton UP, 1983), translated by H.
and E. Hong, 42 fn.
[39] Kierkegaard, *Training in Christianity* (Vintage, 2004), 83; emphasis
added.

annihilate the miscreants ... I advent Myself millennium after millennium," just as we know the miscreants have and are rewriting history to paint themselves as victims and heroes and are dictating governmental policies (through pure decree or the manipulation of public opinion via the same media they control) that will inevitably lead to the marginalization and erasure of Aryan folk. *Terribleness*, then, is a matter of misunderstanding.

Similarly, *wondrousness*, because the events surrounding Hitler's life capture our awe, is a matter of understanding. Both cases demand the sole use of our understanding. However, the understanding is incapable of taking the next step: engaging the Paradox. For when the understanding reaches the point of confrontation, the offense appears. "I am offended that Hitler was a great man"; "I am offended that Hitler did good things"; "I am offended that Hitler killed Jews"; "I am offended that Hitler orchestrated the Holocaust"; "I am offended that Hitler was a warmonger"; "I am offended that Hitler manipulated the German people"; "I am offended that you think Hitler is relevant today"; "I am offended that Hitler was God" — such are but some of the offenses taken, of which we see two types: one regarding the nature of the man, one regarding the supposed actions of the man.

Both types of offense must be confronted given the morass of complexity fabricated in the postwar world; in the case of Hitler's nature, we must believe or be offended by the Führer's fundamental goodness and his appearance as God; in the case of Hitler's alleged actions, we must believe or be offended by both the revisions and allegations concerning Adolf Hitler, and by the Führer's compulsion to do what's demanded by divine restoration, which is related to the first type of offense. The facticity of many offenses aside, all any proofs can do is bring us to the point of decision: it is at this point we must decide to believe or be offended. That is, we are confronted with the limits of understanding: the Paradox.

Kierkegaard offhandedly remarks, "Take the paradox away from a thinker and you have a professor," for "the paradox is the passion of thought, and the thinker without the paradox is like the lover without passion: a mediocre fellow."[40] For Kierkegaard, there is no higher existence than that of the faithful, for the faithful have transcended base humanity and communed with God in the *instant* — the moment of confrontation that fuses the temporal and eternal, i.e., the moment of decision. Genuine decision requires the individual passion to surmount the individual and conform to God — all else is cowed complicity, inauthenticity. Thus, the Paradox is essential for authentic humanity. One cannot meet the Paradox without the possibility of offense: "He who believes must, *in order to attain faith*, have passed through the possibility of the offense."[41] This must be emphasized: *Faith is not possible without the offense.* "The possibility of offense is just the repellent force by which faith comes into existence..."[42] The offense forces the individual into a position of authenticity: become attentive through proofs; engage the Paradox — i.e., the limits of understanding; choose to believe and undertake your first authentic act, or choose to remain offended and continue an uninspired existence.

I am offended that Hitler... — this is the precipice of faith. With a thoughtful choice, one can wrest from mechanized existence genuine freedom. The choice is only a moment, however, flashing across a canvas leaden with customary quips and pithy slogans repeated in an endless, monotonous drone. Doctrinairism's pull is easy to abide: one needn't think at all! Heed the horde and fade into the mucked and dreary background: continue a life of unbothered agitation, mixed into a muddle of meaninglessness *for all time.* But this is not the language of the Avatāra; his is the language of *duplexity*, which is to say, the language of thought. The advent of the Avatāra, the herald from the vacuum, was dualistic, not in essence, but in sense: God is God until God is man; then God is the offense, the precipice of faith. It is not God who changes, but the one facing the offense: "faith itself has a dialectical quality — and the receiver is the one who is revealed, whether he will believe or

---

[40] *Philosophical Fragments* (Princeton UP, 1987), "The Absolute Paradox," translated by H. and E. Hong.

[41] Kierkegaard, *Training in Christianity* (Vintage, 2004), 87.

[42] Kierkegaard, *Training in Christianity* (Vintage, 2004), 107.

be offended."[43] When confronted with the Paradox, one is "in a completely solitary position, without any support whatsoever."[44]

From this position, one must choose to see the Godhead for what he is — or be offended. This solitary position is *everything* to us: it is *struggle, freedom,* and *life*. We must be grateful for the existence of Adolf Hitler, for his life compels us to confront ourselves. His "Archetype is an extra-cosmic poem writing itself on this Earth through the heroes of both sexes, those who deliver their lives like a blank page so that He may write his redemptive immortal poems on them."[45] And if we open ourselves to the *cosmic muse*, the "extra-cosmic poem," then we earn the envy of the gods; for, unlike the faithful who remain behind in this darkest of ages, "full of awful shadows," the gods haven't the chance to make the leap, to sacrifice themselves for the Supreme Creator, for the Myth of the Blood. The remaining faithful continue the struggle against all odds — *nonetheless.*[46] In Hitler Avatāra we have locus; in rejection of the choice, we are lost. That the choice exists at all is a testament to God's divine order.

For the faithful, the choice is simple: being an individual with freedom is invaluable; this is not *despite* the outcome that exercising real individual freedom results in conformity with the transcendent, but *because of* it. Freedom only exists in God, in faith; the offense makes it possible.

> Without the death-struggle which is the birth-throe of faith, without the shudder which is the first experience of worship, without the dread of the possibility of offense, one learns to know directly that which cannot be known directly.[47]

---

[43] Kierkegaard, *Training in Christianity* (Vintage, 2004), 125.

[44] Kierkegaard, *Training in Christianity* (Vintage, 2004), 127.

[45] Serrano, *Adolf Hitler: The Ultimate Avatar* (Hermitage Helm, 2014), 203.

[46] Serrano, *Adolf Hitler: The Ultimate Avatar* (Hermitage Helm, 2014), 195.

[47] Kierkegaard, *Training in Christianity* (Vintage, 2004), 120.

Kierkegaardian Christianity is really just Germanicism — i.e., it is the Aryan approach to life: meaning through struggle, light emerging from the dark. What Kierkegaard saw in Christianity was only a reflection of his own Germanic soul, much like Rembrandt's perfection of chiaroscuro was a reflection of *his* Germanic soul.[48] When he says that without faith and the possibility of offense, "one learns to know directly that which cannot be known directly," he implicitly extols the transcendent, which is to say, *Germanicism*. Faith and the possibility of offense both predicate and are predicated by the Paradox, which is to say, *that which cannot be known directly*. One cannot "know directly that which cannot be known directly," for if this were the case, we would no longer have passion and the subtle intimacy with the transcendent (Godhead), but rather the crude understanding of modernity or, as Kierkegaard is wont to say, "paganism."

This "paganism," it must be stressed, is not akin to, say, Germanic heathenry, but rather the techno-mechanical, scientific understanding of the modern world: it is a de-spiritualized approach to existence, wherein the ineffable is a mere condition for parody. In short, without the desire to commune with the unknowable, we would simply be replacing sublime Gothic spires and majestically adorned domes with the dull concrete of equitable housing blocks.

Life without faith, at best, is a drab mediocrity. Faith is freedom; faith is inspiration; faith gives fire to the struggle and the struggle gives meaning to life; without it, we have no choice but to live mired in ignorance — despite how educated we imagine we are — because when we were confronted with the limits of understanding, we took affront and turned back, once and for all — just the same as everyone else. Such a dreary existence is ripe for the Judeo-harvest, the mass enslavement of the Aryan folk for all time. Make no mistake: the Jews want you faithless and adrift: Aryan faithlessness is key to Jewish supremacy, for *the faithless man does not fight*. To Jews and their acolytes, you are a number. To God, you are *der Freiheitskämpfer*, and an essential part of the Paradox that stands as Aryan redemption.

---

[48] For more on this, see Julius Langbehn's *Rembrandt as Educator*.

"This, then, is the ultimate paradox of thought," Kierkegaard instructs: "to want to discover something that thought itself cannot think."[49] We cannot think of the Paradox, for it is beyond the limits of our knowledge. We therefore must make the leap of faith that carries us to God. Faith, however, is not a *bridge* but a *break*: it does not span the gulf from known to unknown, but stops the known from going one step further. Acknowledging the "paradox of thought" makes us *thoughtful* so that we may be *unthinking*; that is, to reach the Paradox we must be *aware, conscientious, thoughtful* — but we must not think, for thinking precludes communion with God. Thoughtfulness, or mindfulness, imbues our life and action with the meaning necessary to *fight* and thus *realize* what it means to be fully human: that humanity without God is mere biological machinery destined for drab mediocrity. This thoughtfulness brings us to the brink: we must now choose to believe or be offended. If we believe in that which "proofs might serve to make a man attentive," then we have broken with the drab mediocrity of biological machinery: we are on the path to positively contributing to the Cosmic Struggle, for we are filled with the faith necessary to secure our freedom and inspire our descendants, sowing "the seed of life from which, one day, a new tree will strike firm root."[50]

We embark alone, full of courage, and will thereby commune with the courageous of all eras. We greet the unknown as the light of our salvation, for it frees us from the binds of an understanding warped under the weight of demiurgical darkness: "[The unknown] is the absolutely different in which there is no distinguishing mark. [It] seems to be at the point of being disclosed, but not so, because the understanding cannot even think the absolutely different..."[51] It is for precisely this reason that the defendants at Nuremberg were seen to be *Martians*: "Two worlds confronted one another, with no means of communication. It was like trying to judge creatures from

---

[49] *Philosophical Fragments* (Princeton UP, 1987), "The Absolute Paradox."
[50] Clausewitz, *Political Testament* (1812).
[51] Kierkegaard, *Philosophical Fragments* (Princeton UP, 1987), "The Absolute Paradox."

Mars by the standards of our humanist civilization...."[52] And it is through this faithful *break* that we are joined with our kinsmen in undying faith:

> I regret nothing. If I were to begin all over again, I would act again just as I have acted — even if I knew that I would meet a fiery death at the stake. No matter what people may do or say, one day I shall stand before the judgment seat of eternal God. I will answer to Him, and he will vindicate me.[53]

There is no death, but only the unknown. Death is what overtakes us when we bow to an *understanding* we fail to realize is a means of Judeo-control. Conversely, the unknown is what binds us to the Eternal, it is the self which is a "relation relating to itself."[54] Faith stops the known from going *one step further*. In another realm the Führer received the warning: *Go as far as to retake your colonies and not one step further!* Meaning, *do not invade the Soviet Union.*[55] This, however, was an *understanding* trying to stop *faith*. Adolf Hitler knew the consequences of undertaking *Barbarossa*, but he was fated to propel the war *further into the unknown*:

> Hitler himself was to be carried away on the currents of Destiny, by the powerful prevailing Winds of the almighty *Avatar*, and already He could do or change

---

[52] Louis Pauwels and Jacques Bergier, *Morning of the Magicians* (Avon Books, 1972), 257-258. The following statement from Pauwels (a Jew) appears in the same discussion on the stark differences between Hitlerism and the Judeo-ideologies of the Allies: "One can quite well imagine Marxism and liberalism coexisting, because they are based on the same kind of ideas, and belong to the same Universe" (258). Indeed they are and indeed they do; they are two sides of the same Jewish coin that allied against Hitlerism to slaughter millions of Aryans from all combatants.

[53] Rudolf Hess' final statement before the Nuremberg Tribunal.

[54] Kierkegaard, *The Sickness unto Death* (Penguin, 2004), translated by Alistair Hannay, 43.

[55] As recorded in Serrano's *The Golden Thread, The Ultimate Avatar*, and *Manu*.

nothing. He said this to his adjutant, Krause, at the moment of attack against Poland: "I can no longer do anything to control events, much less stop them. Not even I know how this will end..." Thus spoke Hitler, the man.[56]

And thus from the beginning was faith precipitated. *Barbarossa* was inevitable from September 1939. Faith was inevitable from 1889 — faith *within* the Cosmic Struggle, which is necessary for perpetuating Aryandom and final victory. *We embark alone, full of courage, and will thereby commune with the courageous of all eras. We regret nothing.* But we know how our encounter with the unknown ends: *We arrive at the mystery of all beginning.* Thus lives Hitler Avatāra.

∞ ∞ ∞

The paradox of thought brings us to *the* Paradox — the point of offense at which we must break with understanding or be damned. How can a man be God? How can the *infinite* manifest as the *finite*? How could a man who acted so incongruously to accepted ethical standards be God? *Are we not offended?*

So inseparable from faith is the possibility of offense that if the God-Man were not the possibility of offense, He could not be the object of faith... For if the possibility of offense were lacking, direct communication would be in place, and thus the God-Man would be an idol. Direct recognizableness is paganism.[57]

For Kierkegaard, the reason being a Christian had become "in the modern view ... as [simple and] direct as putting the foot into the stocking" and Christianity itself had been "done away with"[58] is because Christianity *never existed in the first place*: the Germanic

---

[56] Serrano, *Manu* (Hermitage Helm, 2017), 38.
[57] Kierkegaard, *Training in Christianity* (Vintage, 2004), 128.
[58] Kierkegaard, *Training in Christianity* (Vintage, 2004), 111-112 (and 30-31).

world *could not* be Christian in in the Kierkegaardian sense — that is, the *Germanic* sense — because they lacked offense at Christ — that is, there existed no real faith, but only *understanding*. Kierkegaard recognized two ways in which offense at Christ might occur: (1) one would take offense at the fact that a mere man — and Christ was indeed a man to those contemporary with him — proclaims himself to be God, and (2) one would take offense at the lowly station of a supposed God on earth.[59] Because European Christendom did not place itself contemporary with Christ — imagining itself as living side by side with a poor, unknown "carpenter's son" — it could only be enamored with an assured Christ-King and the pre-Christian (i.e., *indigenous*) traditions that Judeo-Christianity had overwritten (e.g., *Ostern, Jul,* and the salvific and empowering life of Wotan) and was thusly content in a pre-established Victory of the Cross.

Remember that to be "pagan" for Kierkegaard is, in essence, only to have a simplistic, matter-of-fact *understanding* of the "divine" (which is to say, *idolatry*); "direct communication" is our greatest peril because it occludes the mystery — the unknown, the Paradox. The only way to thwart "direct communication" is through the thoughtfulness that brings us to the edge of understanding — that is, through *faith*. Mystery, the irrational, the mystic power of Nature — these are what crown our humanity. But this is not what Christian missionaries brought with them on their treks through northern Europe; instead, they brought their "direct communication": *Accept the body and blood of Christ, Northman, because he reflects what you revere in Nature and the gods — that is, what you revere in yourself!* With this, the missionaries won more tithes for *Roma* and the Germanics understood how to expand their influence by better integrating into a Semiticized Roman society.

What was lost, of course, was *Deutschtum* for all time: discarding that which was fundamentally German, or Aryan, from Germanic belief led only to a waywardness which reverberates to this day — now we are faced with faithless floating, we are anchorless

---

[59] Kierkegaard, *Training in Christianity* (Vintage, 2004), 70.

and adrift, plodding the path of drab mediocrity to Jewish enslavement, smothered in the dark of a blackened canvas.

Our salvation is the offense and that which waits beyond it. That we might be offended at Hitler Avatāra makes faith possible. That the Jews and their acolytes might be offended at Hitler Avatāra affirms Aryan life. Let us consider the "accepted ethical standards" that Hitler so frankly abandoned. We again recall the words of Krishna Avatāra, the eighth manifestation of the Godhead: *To deliver the pious and to annihilate the miscreants ... I advent Myself millennium after millennium.*[60] "Accepted ethical standards" is euphemism for *formally sanctioned miscreant mayhem*. God manifests to right the wrongs of a world upturned. If the faithless and godless degenerates are offended at one who seeks a restoration of Nature's divine justice, we should rejoice! Right is revealed in the miscreants' offense.

Kierkegaard, too, speaks of a *teleological suspension of the ethical*: In one's absolute duty to God, it is divine command that supplants any ethical norms. Here, then, we have two ways of interpreting "accepted ethical standards": (1) the ethical standards and those who establish and enforce them are precisely the problem leading the world into catastrophe and must therefore be expunged (*vernichten*), and (2) despite any ethical standards, one beholden to divine diktat must act in accordance with the will of God. The first interpretation points to the "proofs [that] might serve to make a man attentive"; the second interpretation, however, is the hour of decision that propels us into the transcendent. While we can perceive, experience, hypothesize, and test Nature's order, and thus deliver verifiable conclusions about its harmony, questions inevitably arise regarding the validity of the so-called *absolute duty to God* given its subjective nature.

Such questions, however, are asked in vain, for objective validity is precisely what's left behind after the break between theoretically rational understanding and irrational faith. It is this departure from the "objective" and "understanding" that creates the *moment* of authenticity, and thus freedom, for man; this moment

---

[60] Bhagavad Gita IV.8.

must be fought for and won time and again for as long as one lives, which is the condition, the *toll*, of freeing faith. *Freedom* for the subject — or subjectivity — is predicated on faith. It is only through extracting oneself from the universal (condition of the ethical), as a thoughtful, conscientious, and aware individual within the universal (condition of the ethical) that one might approach the Paradox and thus face the possibility of offense and authenticity.

> *Through the individual's intercourse with himself the individual is made pregnant by himself and gives birth to himself.* The self the individual knows is simultaneously the actual self and the ideal self, which the individual has outside himself as the image in whose likeness he is to form himself, and which on the other hand he has within himself, since it is he himself....
>
> When the individual has known himself and has chosen himself, he is in the process of actualizing himself, but since he is supposed to do that freely, he must know what it is he wants to actualize. What he wants to actualize is certainly himself, but it is his ideal self, which he cannot acquire anywhere but within himself.... What is required of [him] is the universal; what [he is] able to do is the particular. Yet this skepticism has great significance, ... as it shows that *the personality itself is the absolute.*
>
> But this must be defined more closely. Curiously enough, language itself points up this skepticism. I never say of a man: He is doing duty or duties; but I say: He is doing *his* duty; I say: I am doing *my* duty, do *your* duty. This shows that the individual is simultaneously the universal and the particular. Duty is the universal; it is required of me. Consequently, if I am not the universal, I cannot discharge the duty either. On the other hand, *my duty* is the particular, something for me alone, and yet it is duty and consequently the universal. Here personality appears in its highest validity. It is not lawless; neither does it itself establish its

> law, for the category of duty continues, but *the person-*
> *ality takes the form of the unity of the universal and the*
> *particular....*
>
> The fundamental point, therefore, is not whether a
> person can count on his fingers how many duties he
> has, but that he has once and for all felt the intensity of
> duty in such a way that the consciousness of it is for
> him the assurance of the eternal validity of his being.[61]

The ethical, generally, is not something to be spurned; it is the underlying condition of society and presents us the possibility of self-
actualization through our own ethical duty. However, when the
underlying conditions of society are spurned by those who seek to
thwart the natural order from which the ethical arises for selfish,
exploitative gain, then our duty becomes the *ousting* of the prevailing (un)ethical order; this coincides with the above-listed first interpretation. That "the personality itself is the absolute" ties the
first interpretation to the second, for it is the *internal* ("unity of the
universal and the particular") that orients us to the *external* (uni-
versal/ethical), and never vice versa. This internal duty — felt in
quality ("intensity"[62]), not *quantity* — assures us of the eternal validity of our being, for *from ourselves* do we see our relation to that
which has created us: "the primary question ... is always that a person with respect to his own life is not his uncle but his father" —
this is how *Through the individual's intercourse with himself the in-*
dividual is made pregnant by himself and gives birth to himself.

    We see in ourselves, with all the reverence and intensity of the
Absolute, the Absolute Law that created us. This does not mean, as
would be the case in a Nihilistic sense, that we partake in any sor-
did self-worship; rather, it means that we see in ourselves a window
to the Eternal, the Divine Order of Nature: God speaks *to* us
through us. Therefore, our absolute duty to God is our absolute duty to each other; we are remiss if we ignore *the unity of self and uni-*

---

[61] Kierkegaard, *Either/Or*, Part II, "Development of the Personality" (II
141); emphasis added.
[62] Kierkegaard, *Either/Or*, Part II: "it is not a matter of the *multiplicity* of
duty but of its *intensity*..." — emphasis added.

versal that is our own being — a being that, if we are thoughtful, attentive, and conscientious, is brimming with the intensity of absolute quality. And so it is that the particular becomes the universal and the universal becomes the particular: it is written in our own being.

Thus, although its source is the inscrutable self, the absolute duty to God to restore rightness in an (un)ethical world is itself the ultimate ethical approach. Paradoxically, this is despite the fact that seeking an understanding of the subject in the context of the objective-universal is a Sisyphean task.[63] And if this adds to the possibility of offense, so much the better: We can be certain that the divine path is squarely underfoot, precisely as Kierkegaard augured.

In identifying the link between the necessity of the offense and the possibility of faith as essential properties of God, as well as in recognizing the inherent relationship between faith and struggle, Kierkegaard anticipated the being-event of Hitler Avatāra; that is, the great Germanic thinker *revealed the underlying mythos of a free existence*. In this way, Kierkegaard was a prophet of Hitlerism; his rebukes of Christianity were not appeals for reformation, but calls for revolution. Christendom — and thus Europe — was sick with contentment: lacking offense at Christ and taking his godhood as granted shackled the European spirit. Aryan Europe was not *free from understanding* and, thus, *free in faith*; it was coerced into a lightless enslavement to Judeo-Christianity through sword and swindle. But Aryan Europe *could not* have *faith* in Christ, for Christ was superimposed over pre-existing beliefs.[64] Kierkegaard, then, was not attempting to extract from Aryandom an impossible faith in the Jewish Christ, but was rather clearing the way for a faith in

---

[63] It is quite telling that many of the same people who would hesitate to accept faith in Adolf Hitler's (*Germanic*) attempt to construct an exoteric/esoteric Reich *protecting* Germanic people *for all time* are, in fact, the same people who readily accept Abraham's (*Jewish*) commitment to murder his only son — all in the name of an absolute duty to God. The Jewish reach is indeed far, and insidious *White Traitors*, the most zealous of all Jew-collaborators, are everywhere.

[64] See Guido von List's *The Transition from Wotanism to Christianity* and James Russell's *The Germanization of Early Medieval Christianity*.

an anticipated Germanicism — one in which *offense* could be taken and the *struggle for faith* could free Aryandom from servitude *for all time.*

Carl Jung identified the stunted development of Germanic consciousness ensuing from the alien infiltration of Christianity into Europe.[65] Germanic heathenry did not become fully realized, and thus the Germanic spirit was also inhibited. The *struggle for faith* is so absolutely essential because from it culture arises. That the Germanic folk are so intensely individualistic is a testament to their firm and organic proclivity to piety: their belief in themselves and the causes they uphold is only a reflection of their belief in the transcendent Creator. This attitude lends itself to the "artistic-intellectual" spirit which distinguishes the Germanic people as "the artistically most significant of all peoples."

Thus Aryan passion is Aryan expression. We create and strive because we are *from* the Creator. Culturally, spiritually — *racially* — faith is our natural state. When Christianity arrived in Europe, our inborn faith was supplanted by the predetermined Victory of the Cross, and this, in turn, precluded our natural development as a people of faith. Scheming and universalistic ecumenicalism took the place of race as the bedrock of Aryan existence. The Aryan became focused not on cultural expression, but rather on the indoctrinating effects of institutionalization. With Christianity, the hive-mind of the Orient entered Aryandom,[66] and thus was stunted, as Jung describes, the development of the European folk.

The history of embattled Europe, then, is a history of the antagonistic dynamic of alien Christianity groping for fulfillment

---

[65] "The Western world 'was interrupted in its development from paganism through the imposition of another culture.' Without a doubt he was referring to Christianity." — Jung, as quoted in Miguel Serrano's *Son of the Widower* (Hermitage Helm, 2013), 23.

[66] Adolf Hitler fought ceaselessly to repel this hive-mind, which was later manifest in liberal-democratic parliamentarianism, and to restore Germanic individualism: "We deceive ourselves if we believe that the people want to be governed by majorities.... This people does not wish to lose itself in *majorities*.... It wants a leadership in which it can believe, nothing more" (21 August 1927 [speech]).

amongst a folk yearning for their native voice as faithful individuals. The martial European attitude is the result of this hindered spiritual development and the inborn, freedom-loving individualism sparking creative, conquering urges. Native European attitudes have been exploited and pressed by Jewish manipulation, for Demiurge-Jehovah-Satan lusts for human blood, particularly the blood of non-Jews.[67] Immense wars, unrest, and their embers are constantly smoldering on the Continent and its colonial progeny, the stoked aim of which is Jewish-orchestrated division, instability, and the harvest of Aryan blood to quench Judeo-bloodlusts. Jewish plots will in the near future issue yet another massive war in which Europe is at the very center; this will not only satiate satanic Judeo-bloodlusts and eliminate masses of European stock, but will also create exploitable opportunities for war profiteering — not just in the capital-enterprise sense, but also in the racial sense, as the societal holes in European societies will now "need" to be filled with "economic migrants" from Africa and Asia.[68] Money and power are

---

[67] For examples of Jewish manipulation, see the works of Joseph Goebbels, Alfred Rosenberg, Thomas Dalton, Henry Ford, Martin Luther, etc.
[68] Two-time Medal of Honor recipient and former general Smedley Butler observed,

> The normal profits of a business concern in the United States are six, eight, ten, and sometimes twelve percent. But wartime profits — *ah! that is another matter* — twenty, sixty, one hundred, three hundred, and even eighteen hundred per cent — the sky is the limit. All that traffic will bear. Uncle Sam has the money. Let's get it. Of course, it isn't put that crudely in wartime. It is dressed into speeches about patriotism, love of country, and 'we must all put our shoulders to the wheel,' but the profits jump and leap and skyrocket — and are safely pocketed.

Butler lamented such war profiteering in 1935 ("War is a Racket"); the problem has only worsened since then. Business profits of defense contractors of the Military Industrial Complex aside, accountability of funds is notoriously difficult to track in times of conflict. Hundred- or thousand-paged spending bills are rammed through Congress throwing billions toward this or that "existential threat to democracy." Legislators, let alone the public, have little idea of how each cent is being used. It is

the twin lusts of the golems and their Satan-Jehovah, and the go-lems interfere at every turn to ensure their increase.

Conversely, creativity drives the Aryan, and from this creativity comes divine culture, which is an expression of inborn faith: the struggle for faith is the struggle for freedom; the faithful fight is cul-ture's source. For whom do we fight? Now we fight for the MAN TO COME.

The MAN TO COME is born of struggle and is the spiritual-cultural expression of a beleaguered folk. This struggle is the para-dox of thought and Paradox of being that stands as the native state of Aryandom.

> We know that the father of all things is combat and struggle. We see that race is of supreme importance to the life of our nation as well as character, the basis of which must be responsibility toward our folk. We are absolutely convinced that every decision requires re-sponsibility. That is why we are at odds with the entire world, that is why we are considered subversive and why we are prohibited from speaking, and that is why we are silenced — because we want to restore the health of our entire German nation...[69]

Firstly, and notably, Adolf Hitler here marks *character* as having equal weight with *race*. This fact of Hitlerism is often, if not always, conveniently ignored by detractors, as a typical tactic of theirs is to fabricate a "Nazi" straw man who imagines that "race is everything" and "white people are always good," a position that can be easily demolished upon encountering the first white miscreant. Hitler's Reich handled such reprobates the same any other: concentrate them in a *work* camp and remind them that *Arbeit macht frei* —

---

money laundering at its finest. Not only this, but billions "mysteriously" turn up missing (for but one example, recall Rumsfeld's reaction to the trillions gone missing on the eve of 9/11 — convenient, too, how such a story would understandably get completely forgotten after a 9/11-type event). Harmless accidents, no doubt.
[69] Adolf Hitler, echoing Heraclitus, 18 January 1927 (speech).

surmount your weakness in character through *struggle*. Hitlerists rather believe that *race* is the bedrock of spiritual-cultural expression, but *character* ultimately determines *value* or *quality*.

Adolf Hitler, echoing Heraclitus, reminds us that struggle is the "father of all things" — it is the father of spiritual-cultural expression, which is individual freedom for the Aryan. *Struggle* means birth and death, creation and destruction — it is Brahma and Shiva; it is also Vishnu: preservation, or restoration, of the Good that has waned. *Struggle* is the Aryan's approach to the precipice of understanding and the faithful leap to salvation on the other side: it is the definition of his being and the reflection of his God; it is that which distinguishes him among all the peoples of this world. Faith is born of struggle and the struggle is born of faith.

> We National Socialists therefore make the holy promise never to rest in raising the honor of [the Swastika] flag, making it our symbol of self-discipline, obedience, and order. Let it be to us a symbol of eternal struggle. We see in this flag the victorious sign of freedom and the purity of our blood. We want this flag to be a symbol of salvation, a sign that faith in these great possessions is alive in our people.[70]

Thus spoke the Führer; thus spoke Hitler Avatāra.

And now we come to the questions, *But how can a man be God? And how can the infinite manifest as the finite?* A man is God when his entire being is set to the task of realizing the will of his folk *for all time* — this is the particular made transcendent; this is the finite made infinite. Paradoxically, as we have seen, it is precisely at this time — when man becomes God — that the man ceases to be; and then we see that the man, the vessel, never existed at all. A man is never God; rather, God on earth is the fulfillment of Nature's order in the blood of a faithful people that God decreed should exist. God, then, is the will of a people to create according to its self-actualizing urge; the Germanic folk — the Aryans — are

---

[70] Adolf Hitler, 21 August 1927 (speech).

preeminent among all folks regarding their creative will. The *Aryans* — the twice born: once in life, once in faith; *they* are the folk destined by God to represent his will on earth; Hitler Avatāra is the Aryan Führer. *As long as this idealism is alive in Germany, Germany shall never die!*[71]

∞ ∞ ∞

"Loyalty to oneself, loyalty to the German soil, loyalty to the German racial spirit — loyalty is the finest German virtue."[72] Loyalty is what makes faith, not just possible, but *inherent* to the Germanic people. Without loyalty, the faithful leap would be inconceivable; without the faithful leap, the Germanic folk would be inconceivable. A faithless German is a Jew, at least in character — hence the obsessive push by the Jews to de-spiritualize (i.e., *deaden*) the Aryan people through godless media, academia (or indoctrination), and government, all while they institutionalize, indoctrinate, and impose a faithless creed of rationalistic Holocaust-guilt on the gullible masses. A faithless Aryan is no Aryan at all, but only another gutless pawn in the Jewish plot. *My honor is loyalty — Meine Ehre heißt Treue*: The SS motto is the Aryan mantra.

Loyalty is woven into Aryan identity; this is why God chooses, time and again, to manifest among the Aryan people. Loyalty surpasses any supposed rationality, for rationality itself is predicated on one's loyalty. We remember Karna. Loyalty is the compulsion of a folk to *stick to their guns*.

> *The type of my disciples.* To such men as *concern me in any way* I wish suffering, desolation, sickness, ill treatment, indignities of all kinds. I wish them to be acquainted with profound self-contempt, with the martyrdom of self-distrust, with the misery of the defeated: I have no pity for them; because I wish them to

---

[71] That is, *as long as this idealism is alive in the Aryan soul, the Aryan folk will never die!* Adolf Hitler, 13 September 1935 (speech).

[72] Julius Langbehn, *Rembrandt as Educator*, "German Character."

have the only thing which today proves whether a man has any value or not, namely, *the capacity of sticking to his guns.*[73]

This is no sadistic wish; this is a call for sincerity — *at all costs*; this is the First Seven of the *Nationalsozialistische Deutsche Arbeiterpartei*; this is the Old Guard of the Hitlerist Revolution.

> It is painful to lose the best of a folk; time and again, the best have always been the ones who have had to meet the enemy in battle. And thus today we also affirm our deepest conviction in the concept of peace; we are mindful of our struggle's difficult sacrifices, but we also couple this love of peace with our resolve to courageously defend the honor and freedom of our nation.... [Now,] I demand that you lay down your lives just as our early martyrs did. *Your lives must have no other purpose but loyalty.* These dead are your examples, and you shall be the unattainable examples for those still to come....[74]

Loyalty is the only path to honor and freedom. From hardship comes hardened steel. Hardship culls the herd of dead weight, of White Traitors, of Seydlitz Troops who want only their daily bread without disturbances. Hardship is the path to freedom because it ignites in those who remain steadfast a will to defend at all costs that which should never be taken for granted: the blood in our veins and our very existence as reflections of our Supreme Creator.

> I appeal in this hour to the entire German folk ... to arm themselves with an even greater, hardened spirit of resistance, until ... we can lay on the grave of the dead of this mighty struggle a wreath with a tie in-

---

73 Nietzsche, *The Will to Power* (B&N, 2006), translated by Anthony Ludovici, Book IV §910.
74 Adolf Hitler, 09 November 1933 (speech).

scribed: *But you have triumphed nonetheless!* I expect every German therefore to fulfill his duty to the utmost, and to take on every sacrifice that will be and must be demanded of him.[75]

Sacrifice and hardship "must be demanded" because without them, a folk ceases to be. No people of any merit or with any view of blood as the link between past, present, and future will avoid or take lightly these twin pillars of faith. Sacrifice undergirds heroism; heroes are both a reflection of a people and a challenge to untested generations to continue the struggle. When the *new* hero is created, the sacrifice is complete. Hardship is the consequence of choosing an authentic life: embrace the hardship of believing in the face of the offense, and welcome the hardship that ensues from a break with the known. When the faithful leap, hardship is both at an end and just beginning. Hitler Avatāra, on the eve of the Reich's material destruction, yet called for loyalty — for it is only loyalty that can carry a folk into the future with renewed strength.

∞ ∞ ∞

In 1453 in a city on the Bosporus, a man named Salvus Salvificus saw two visions of the future. His first vision was of him: He sat alone in his study, at a desk before an open window on a pleasant spring day; a warm breeze carried distant shouts of a foreign tongue. Craning from the window, Salvus saw the sky darken and felt the wind turn cold; the shouts drew nearer, but were no longer indecipherable; he heard the voices saying, "Take and eat, this is my body..." Descending from the window, as if floating, Salvus met one of the swarthy, foreign-tongued visitors in the street, and Salvus spoke: "Take and drink, this is my blood..." The two strangers clasped arms and entered a nearby church; outside, screams were muffled in the cold wind... The second vision was an enigma: Two figures, each dressed in black and each bearing a torch, stood facing one another in a lightless abyss. Both figures used their torches

---

[75] Adolf Hitler, 30 January 1945 (speech).

to try and uncover what the abyss had consumed. One figure, a bent old man with cruel eyes and a chilling scowl, wore a rabbi's garb, dark and dreadful. A young man — healthy and strong, fair skinned, with light hair and eyes — stood opposite the rabbi; his was a kind of uniform, sleek and unusual. On the collar were two zigzagged lines of white, like lightning. The rabbi spoke an alien dialect, but Salvus understood: "When the tree crosses your way, we will have won. When we cross your way, you will have one." Benighted, the young man thundered, "When you've one, Purim comes! When we've won, we will as strangers run!" With this the two figures threw aside their torches and the abyss alighted with the collared lightning.

A warm spring breeze awakened Salvus Salvificus from his trance. In the distance he heard a great disturbance; in the future he saw a great upheaval; in the past he saw a righteousness wrought from foreign tongues. *And above him* — above him he saw a herald from the vacuum illuminating the sky.

Before his blood washed down the gutter, he recorded his visions for posterity.

— 4 —
Faith and Reason

Reason is the means for a man of faith to further the will of God. God's will is the Good. The Good is that which transcends and uplifts; it is sacrificing oneself for the benefit of the whole that reflects oneself; this reflection is physical, mental, and spiritual; the Good is *one thing*.[1] Purity of heart is to will one thing. The Good is singular; it is *willing one thing*. If the will is not singular, purity is lost and one is both confused as to the nature of what is willed[2] and we are distanced from God.

Reason, when it competes with God for supremacy, presents us myriad ends, for each subject necessarily uses reason as a means for subjective ends. When the means become the end, there exist as many ends as there are subjects; that is, what is willed is not one thing. If reason replaces God, then one acts against the Good — for oneself and others.

An individual united in faith *with* and *in* his folk wills one thing: the continued existence and thriving of his blood as it is reflected in his kinsmen. In this context, individual expression is the expression of the whole. Much like in Byzantine iconography where the individual work of art represents a sublime consciousness, each individual in a community of faith is the expression of the transcendent folk. Such work is indelible: Individuality is expressed through the reason meant to further the faith.

The only conceivable community of faith is focused inwardly — on its self, collectively and individually, and thus on God. Faith is pursuant to the offense that demands individual decision, which, in turn, formalizes the Paradox. The Paradox is "the passion of

---

[1] Kierkegaard, *Purity* (Harper, 1956), 54: "The Good without condition and without qualification, without preface and without compromise is, absolutely the only thing that a man may and should will, and is only one thing."

[2] Kierkegaard, *Purity* (Harper, 1956), 55.

thought" that declares "the difference between poetry and reality"[3] — it is the disappearance of the *being* of Hitler into the *state of being* of Hitler Avatāra. The Paradox is the destruction of the good, for the Good cannot exist without its destruction. This means only that "In victory there will be great fame. In defeat, heaven is certain."[4] The Paradox is the thought and loyalty preceding the individual freedom and authenticity a profound decision brings and the subsequent spiritual endurance of a folk. Without individual authenticity, the blood of a people will be lost *for all time*. The *destruction of the individual as a vessel for the supremacy of reason* as both means and end is the salvation of the folk. The Paradox, then, is the necessity of reason to bring about its own end. Faith is individual reason identifying its limit and sublimating itself into the means of its destruction (the offense) for the furtherance of supra-individual ends — that is, the will of God.

Faith is the Paradox. Without faith, reason loses all meaning — we become awash in the glut of inauthentic personalities pursuing selfish ends; that is to say, we become awash in reason. *Without* faith, reason is both means *and* end, which is to say, it is *neither* and rather like the "and" linking "means and end" but devoid of the meaning of either "means" or "end." *With* faith, reason is *means* and faith is *end*. We use reason to see the proofs that might serve to make us attentive[5]; we use faith to exalt self and folk, which is to say, God, the *one thing*. In the exaltation, we take care not to turn the authenticity of individual choice into a doctrine, for then we are on the path to reason supplanting God, then we are on the path to material-aristocracy supplanting spiritual-aristocracy.

One may choose faith and break with understanding, or one may choose to be offended. Choosing *faith* is an authentic choice, for one uses reason to become freed of blind reason, i.e., the unthinking conformity with godless, materialistic lifeways bereft of spiritual-cultural awareness. Choosing to be *offended*, on the other hand, is really no choice at all, for one simply *rejects* the moment of

---

[3] Kierkegaard, *Philosophical Fragments* (Princeton UP, 1987), "The Absolute Paradox" and *Training in Christianity* (Vintage, 2004), 58.

[4] Mahabharata, Karna Parva, §84.

[5] Kierkegaard, *Training in Christianity* (Vintage, 2004), 83.

decision — i.e., the moment of authenticity — altogether and thus remains in a kind of suspended conformist animation: one is mere automaton, blind to the links between individual action and collective destiny.

Faith and its concomitant authenticity stand as both cultural markers and the requisites for a folk's endurance. The faithful commune with God — i.e., their authentic self as it relates to both itself and the blood from which it arises — and become the raw material for heroic action aimed at perpetuating God through the Myth of the Blood, which is our salvation. Hitler Avatāra *advented* to remind us of the divine harmony that created us and unmask the Malefic Jew that seeks our degradation and enslavement.

Be offended and choose. Salvation hangs suspended in the chasm. You must leap to get it.

∞ ∞ ∞

Every revolution is concretized with blood. This is Nature's law. Incredible plate tectonics form new landmasses; devastating storm fronts bring balance and fair weather; agonizing childbirth welcomes new love. Each night portends a new dawn. *Night is not less wonderful than day — it is equally the work of God; it is lit by the splendor of the stars and reveals to us things that the day does not know.*[6] Fear not what approaches *nonetheless*. Where reason balks, faith embraces. And despite its undeniable power, reason is often left groping in the dark; what leads us to the next morning is the trust we have in our kin and will, which is to say, the faith we have in our future.

Old and current orders wish to divide, and this they do; we are worse because of it. Parlor tricks dazzle the eye and feign unity where there are only haughty, hollow abstractions, where there are only imperious uniforms, where there exists only a common language. *Bloodless superficialities!* — Reason groping in the dark. But faith nudges us in the right direction. When abstractions betray

---

[6] Nikolai Berdyaev, *The End of Our Time* (Semantron, 2009), translated by Donald Attwater, 71.

you, when uniforms are gone, when tongues go silent, what is left? *The blood in your veins remains.* Race is not everything, but it is the beginning of everything; this is the Myth of the Blood, which is the mystery of all beginning. Faith in and loyalty to our folk will carry us to the New Order. Kinfolk are comrades — a family united in struggle, united in creation. As long as our folk abides, so too does our will. Where the Judeo-World Order seeks to destroy, we will create, as is our nature. We can only create when we stay true to each other; when our history and vision are shared, so will be our victory.

Reason is the means for the man of faith to further the will of God. In a godless world, the will of God is always revolutionary. *Gott mit uns!* — because it is God that courses in our veins.

— 5 —
Contemporaneousness:
A Clarion Call

Contemporaneousness is key to authenticity. It is essential for both the offense and the mindfulness preceding the break with understanding. One must see oneself as contemporary with that which causes offense in order to be offended and positioned for the fateful decision.

Kierkegaard spoke of being contemporary with Christ as the only means by which one might attain faith and, thus, everlasting life.

> We look back to those beautiful times [when Christ lived]. Sweet sentimental longing leads us to the goal of our desire, to see Christ walking about in the promised land. *We forget the anxiety, the distress, the paradox....* Was it not terrifying that this man walking around among the others was God? Was it not terrifying to sit down and eat with him? Was it such an easy matter to become an apostle? But the result, the eighteen centuries — that helps, that contributes to this mean deception whereby *we deceive ourselves and others.*[1]

Contemporaneousness is both mental and spiritual struggle: One must wrestle with the immense task of *placing oneself* in the time of the offense. This is no child's play, no mere imagining. One must experience the *absurdity* of believing the *unbekannter Mann* is God, that the *mere man* is God.[2] In the case of Christ, "It is 1,800 years

---

[1] Kierkegaard, *Fear and Trembling* (Princeton UP, 1983), 66; emphasis added.
[2] Adolf Hitler spoke often of himself as an *unbekannter Mann* [unknown man]. From 01 May 1937 (speech): "I, too, am a child of this folk, and did not issue from some palace... Neither was I a general; I was a soldier like millions of others. It is a miracle that, here in our country, an unknown man [*unbekannter Mann*] was able to step forth from the army of millions of German people ... to stand at the fore of the Reich and the na-

since Christ lived, so He is forgotten — only His teaching remains
— that is to say, *Christianity has been done away with*."[3] This is to
say that few Christians living today have any idea about what they
"believe" — and this is precisely the point: Christians today *believe*
nothing! Instead, they *know*: they have the luxury of now two millennia at their back wherein the Victory of the Cross is assured —
the splendor of Rome, the centuries of Judeo-Christian Imperium,
papal power, global reach, entwinement with popular consciousness: all these things stand as supposed evidence of Judeo-Christian
truth — but this worldly victory is exactly what has defeated Judeo-
Christian authenticity.

Kierkegaard goes on to argue that one cannot infer a qualita-
tive change in a thing from the consequences of its existence. Regardless of Christ's gradual apotheosization in world-historical fact,
he was "God" all along; it is therefore incumbent upon the astute
believer to *discard* any world-historicity and enter into contemporaneousness with Christ, so that "facts," which alone stand as im-
pediments to faith, might be turned to faith: see what those in the
time immediately following the supposed crucifixion saw, for instance: a world of persecution, a world hostile to Christ *qua* Christ.[4]
Faith is hardly necessary when victory is assured, and such *historical* certitude historicizes and therefore negates the inward decision:
"A historical Christianity is [nonsense] and unchristian confusion."[5]
Not only does this historical certainty preclude the moment of decision (presuming this were possible for the would-be believer in
the first place), but it also implants blasphemous assumptions
within the believer.

---

tion!" From 18 December 1940: "In 1919, I took up a struggle which appeared nearly hopeless at the time. I was an unknown man [*unbekannter
Mann*] who set out to rid a world of resistance, to tear down walls of
prejudice. Prejudice at times is worse than divine force."
[3] Kierkegaard, *Training in Christianity* (Vintage, 2004), 112; emphasis added.
[4] "The blasphemy is what lies at the bottom of the whole undertaking ...
[:] the thought that the consequences of His life are more important
than His life — which effectively is to say that He was a mere man"
(*Training in Christianity* [Vintage, 2004], 24).
[5] Kierkegaard, *Training in Christianity* (Vintage, 2004), 59.

> If [Christ's] glory had been directly visible, so that eve-
> rybody as a matter of course could see it, then it is *false*
> that Christ humbled Himself and took upon Him the
> form of a servant; it is [then] *superfluous* to give warn-
> ing against being offended, for how in the world could
> anybody be offended against glory attired in glory![6]

Christ willed to be, as Kierkegaard puts it, *incognito*. It was God's will to be *unrecognizable* as God — that is, incarnate in the *unbekannter Mann* — so as to prompt the grave decision. Thus, presuming Jesus was recognizable as God or that one would undoubtedly have known his identity had one lived contemporaneously with him is naught but vanity. Moreover, it is *blasphemy*: the Christian perhaps supposes that he would have guessed Christ's identity despite God's will to be unrecognizable; this is quite a lot of power for the lowly "believer" — more power than even God.[7]

Christianity has never been more than a *world-historical truth* for the European folk. It was never a faith — as means or an end. It was grafted onto indigenous lifeways and presented as both *factual* and a *reinterpretation* of enduring beliefs.[8] This superimposition interrupted natural European development and inflamed an intra-racial dissonance that has been exploited by Jews through political

---

[6] Kierkegaard, *Training in Christianity* (Vintage, 2004), 60; emphasis added.

[7] Kierkegaard, *Training in Christianity* (Vintage, 2004), 112-117.

[8] Northern European bishoprics often used gentler means of conversion when violence became unfashionable. Bishop Daniel of Winchester urged his missionaries to "at intervals ... compare [the pagans'] superstitions with our Christian doctrines, touching upon them from the flank, as it were, so that the pagans [are] thrown into confusion rather than angered..." Thus the missionaries could exploit the "coincidental similarity between certain Germanic myths, rituals, and symbols and certain Christian religious beliefs, rituals, and symbols." Moreover, Pope Gregory urged King Æthelbert to "suppress the worship of idols, and destroy [pagan] shrines" (Russell, *The Germanization of Early Medieval Christianity* [Oxford UP, 1994], 193, 213, and 185, respectively). The ultimate goal was that the channels of pagan beliefs and places of worship would be preserved but the innards would be Christianized — to make conversion less jarring.

advisement, information control, and the domination of capital both in and outside European lands. Judeo-Christian dissonance fostered suicidal, intra-racial hatred that Jewry easily manipulated for their collective benefit. This not only served to increase Jewry's material wealth and power, but also satisfied — and continues to satisfy — the cosmic debt Jews owe to their master, Demiurge-Jehovah, who lusts for the spiritual power inherent in Aryan blood.[9]

World wars, constant conflict, Middle Eastern turmoil, mass immigration replacing indigenous or predominant European populations, debauched and debased media-entertainment programming, and constant mention of the alleged Holocaust all serve to divide and conquer the will of the Aryan folk. This is Judeo-Christianity's legacy, and all of it stems from the absurd historicity of the alien desert-religion that the Germanic thinker Kierkegaard rightly condemns.

Contemporaneousness is not meant to be an obscure philosophical concept acknowledged on paper but ignored in daily life. It is a wake-up call to any Aryan with sense and soul to see: faith is fundamentally Germanic — it is part of who we are. Our faith is and always has been predicated on our individual self and its place in our community of kinfolk: faith is the *trust* we have in each other, it is the moment of decision when we accept that our *blood* and the deep spiritual-cultural meaning it symbolizes are to be valued more than any materiality. Etymologically, "faith" comes from Old French (i.e., Frankish or Germanic, *feid*) via Latin (*fides*) — *faith in* and *loyalty to* one's family, one's comrades; "trust" likewise comes from the Germanic *traust*, or *traustr*, meaning "strong." Aryans put stock in strong ties — of blood, kin, and character. The divine was and is a reciprocal reflection of trust in the gods and folk-community:

---

[9] Consider for a moment how much of Jewish history revolves around the slaughter of non-Jews. Consider the Jewish holidays that celebrate the spilling of non-Jewish blood. Not only does Passover, for instance, celebrate the ritual murder of non-Jews, it usually falls on or around the Germanic holiday of Easter — a holy time celebrating the return of life (spring) after a long, cold winter. It is no coincidence, and this must be understood and emphasized, that *Germanic holidays celebrate life and Nature* while *Jewish holidays celebrate death and scheming.*

> [The] main functions [of nature and the cosmos] were
> sovereignty and creativity, the latter being manifested
> both in the cosmogony and his paternity in divine and
> human genealogies.... Their gods were close to them,
> [and their attitude toward them was] characterized by:
> 1) awe, and 2) trust, tinged with a certain familiarity.[10]

Indeed, "the cult of the gods was bound to the community."[11] This awe, trust, and familiarity lays the foundation for the faith that can and should be part of our daily life, especially in this world dominated by satanic Jewry and its shabbos-golems, for it frees us, through individual authenticity, of the enslaving shackles of Judeo-materialism.

Contemporaneousness is the means by which we arrive at the offense, and it is through the offense that we arrive at the moment of faith. Kierkegaard was distraught, if not disgusted, by the lack of faith among Christians since they had transformed Christ "fantastically into something other than He is"; his Germanicism stirred from deep within and railed against the godless Christ-believing he saw masquerading as piety, i.e., old Germanic trust.[12] Then, as now, this is no slight against the wayward Aryans duped by Jewish Christianity. Rather, we applaud these good Aryans for instinctively refusing the unnatural Judeo-Christian yoke! Kierkegaard identified the weakness of European Christianity 200 years before the advent of the Avatāra. Unlike Nietzsche with his prophetic anticipation of the *Übermensch*, Kierkegaard did not augur the appearance of God. But though he did not speak directly of the Avatāra, he did anticipate the Germanic folk-belief that came to dominate northern and central Europe both preceding and during Hitler's time: Christianity was an invasive species naturally rejected by its host environment; the native response to this was to turn *inward*, toward *authenticity*, toward a *faith* that imparts meaning, which is to say,

---

[10] Edgar Polomé, ed., *The Indo-Europeans in the Fourth and Third Millennia* (Karoma, 1982), 161-167.

[11] Russell quoting Walter Bäkte, *The Germanization of Early Medieval Christianity* (UNC Press, 1994), 171.

[12] Kierkegaard, *Training in Christianity* (Vintage, 2004), 33.

toward the Aryan community, toward God — outward attachments to the alien historicity of Judeo-Christianity be damned! Kierkegaard felt the longing in his blood for the eventual return of the Germanic folk to its own soul — a soul advented in the *Übermensch*, the collective will of a people oriented on Eternal Nature and manifested in the *state of being* that is Hitler Avatāra.[13]

The Aryan's home is with his folk, with the turn inward. The Aryan Christian, too, is welcome with his kinsmen. But there are conditions to acceptance: one must be fit — physically, mentally, and spiritually; one must be of good character; and one must accept the supremacy of blood in this Judeo-illusion we call the modern world.[14] But note: the stubborn, White Traitor Christian who cannot discard his Jewish master will not be suffered; *the Aryan who refuses to abandon his Jewish creed is worse than the Jew* — for at least the Jew knows he's a Jew.[15] The Victory of the Cross has no merit among Hitlerists: we do not accept oafs, louts, cowards, or any mongrelizing miscreant. One must reject all Jewish indoctrination, the sole purpose of which is to undermine Aryan lifeways through slurs against our ancestors, contemporaries, and descendants. And one must demand, from self and others, the faith that comes with the authentic decision: recognize the Myth of the Blood — recognize yourself and your kinsmen as reflections of a transcendent order — recognize the advantage in the sacrifices you make for the continuation your folk, the continuation of God's will on earth.[16]

------

[13] For more on the *Übermensch as collective will*, see *Myth and Sun: Essays of the ARCHETYPE* (Clemens & Blair, 2022).

[14] See *Myth and Sun: Essays of the ARCHETYPE* (Clemens & Blair, 2022).

[15] What the Christian will never admit, for fear of shattering his whole Jew-infested being, is this: Christianity — like its supposed ideological "enemy," communism — caters "to *all* men of every race, of every civilization, of every tradition, and especially to those who have reasons to feel themselves exploited and downtrodden, *i.e.*, to the immense majority of mankind" (Savitri Devi, *Gold in the Furnace*). This and, of course, that Rabbi Jesus, if he wasn't an invention of Rabbi Saul (Paul), was a Jew.

[16] For more on the Myth of the Blood, see Rosenberg's *Myth of the Twentieth Century* (Clemens & Blair, 2021).

∞ ∞ ∞

Hitler Avatāra was and is the speaker for the rights of free peoples to survive and thrive; these rights spring from the faith individuals of the same blood have in themselves and their communities, the necessity of race as the foundational spiritual-cultural element, and the appearance of a folk's will both temporally and transcendently. The temporal manifestation of Aryan will existed in Adolf Hitler, whose historicity is the proof that might serve to make one attentive to the moment of transcendent decision wherein the Avatāra arises. Hitler Avatāra is the ultimate expression of the Germanic will-to-live and therefore the pinnacle of Aryan faith. Faith in Hitler Avatāra and his mission is faith in Aryan existence *for all time*, which is to say, it is faith in God. Faith is all the more necessary in a world ruled by Darkness; Aryan faith is the light of our Supreme Creator emerging from the shadows. Hitlerists *live* the difficulties other creeds can only *imagine* as they celebrate their own *Victories of the Cross. Contemporaneousness* is the Hitlerist's *reality* and sets the conditions for future triumph.

The vanity of the victors has defined the world since 1945; and even before *Götterdämmerung*, the Jews and their golems were celebrating victory over the Germanic world as the Reich was carved up one knowing smile at a time in Tehran. No matter how far back in history one looks, however, one will find Jews running amok, trying like the hellfire that spawned them to parasitize and usurp; their most common host, because he is their chief enemy, is the Aryan.

Hence we see the greatest number of expulsions of Jews come from Aryan lands. Should you ask them why they have so often been targeted for expulsion, Jews will doubtlessly offer some woeful tale of *unwarranted persecution* — such an unfortunate people! Misfortune has not stopped their scheming, however. Not only are they terribly "unfortunate," but it is now the Aryans who expelled them who are the "bigoted tyrants"! Naturally, the Jews did nothing wrong. And with Jewish control pervading European-stock societies, the "Jew = victim" narrative continues. It is used to browbeat Aryans into submission and as means to garner more guilt-prompted power. Criticize Jews and one is immediately labeled an "anti-Semite" — a tactic even former Israeli Prime Minister Shulamit Aloni conceded: "It's a trick — we always use it! When from Europe somebody is criticizing Israel, we bring up the Holocaust; when in [the United States] people are criticizing Israel, then they are 'anti-Semitic.'"[17] Jews use this deception, along with their expanding inventory of "hate speech" laws, to silence their detractors and incrementally increase their stranglehold on world affairs. Perhaps Aloni would draw a distinction between criticizing "Israel" and criticizing "the Jews," but the crucial point remains: Jews admittedly use deception to justify nefarious actions — i.e., attack their enemies and distract others. Jews have used this stratagem for their entire existence: their very identity rests upon the notion that they are a people unjustly "victimized" and "persecuted."[18]

---

[17] *Democracy Now* interview (2002).

[18] Any number of examples could be used to illustrate this. What is perhaps most interesting is that *the Jews' hatred of all things is profound*, even world altering. They ascribe their woes to the very things they hate. Jews constantly allude to "anti-Semitism" and "the Holocaust" because they delight in the hate they fabricate and project; and the Jews want nothing more than to enslave the non-Jews — the *goyim*, the *human-animals* — they despise so much. Here, then, is a typical Jewish jeremiad (2 Esdras 10; NRSVUE):

> Do not do that, but let yourself be persuaded — for how many are the adversities of Zion? — and be consoled because of the sorrow of Jerusalem. For you see how our sanctuary has been laid waste, our altar thrown down, our temple destroyed; our harp has been laid low, our song has been silenced, and our rejoicing has been ended; the light of our lampstand has been put out, the ark of our covenant has been plundered, our holy things have been polluted, and the name by which we are called has been almost profaned; our children have suffered abuse, our priests have been burned to death, our Levites have gone into exile, our virgins have been defiled, and our wives have been ravished; our righteous men have been carried off, our little ones have been cast out, our young men have been enslaved and our strong men made powerless. And, worst of all, the seal of Zion has been deprived of its glory and given over into the hands of those who hate us.

But what is more likely: that the Canaanites, Persians, Philistines, Egyptians, Romans, Russians, Germans, etc. were all supremely evil peoples who "got what they deserved" for "persecuting" the Jews, or that the Jews simply used their usual deception(s) to malign whole peoples and justify their parasitical actions? Similarly, Jewish Prime Minister of Britain Benjamin Disraeli, in his 1844 novel *Coningsby*, boasted, "the world is governed by very different personages from what is imagined by those who are not behind the scenes" — by "personages," of course, he meant the Jews, many of whom he named in the contextual paragraphs. This *shadow government* observation was echoed by the Jew Ed Bernays:

> The conscious and intelligent manipulation of the ... habits and opinions of the masses is an important element in democratic society. Those who manipulate this unseen mechanism of society constitute an invisible government which is the true ruling power of our country.... It is they who pull the wires which control the public mind, who harness old social forces and contrive new ways to bind and guide the world.[19]

That social engineering happens via media and education is clear enough; both now are used, not to inform and educate, but to reinforce the Jew-exalting narrative, the basic schema of which is: Jews are good, "Nazis" are evil, Jews and the Holocaust cannot be ques-

---

Note that these are all things Jews have done, are doing, or would like to do to Germanic Aryans — the world wars are prime cases (the victors, of course, get to both define "war crimes" and decide how they are assigned). Interestingly, and perhaps tellingly, one can scarcely find any instances of Jewish "virgins [being] defiled" or Jewish "wives [being] ravished" — however, one can certainly find many examples of Jewish men defiling and ravishing Aryan women. Consider the "Me Too" movement (c. 2017): several Jewish men, typically Hollywood players, were accused/convicted of abusing an even greater number of, mainly, Aryan women. Consider Weinstein. Consider Epstein.

[19] Edward Bernays, *Propaganda* (Ig Publishing, 2005 [originally published in 1928]), 37-38.

tioned.[20] With this formula and its ceaseless repetition, Jewish supremacy has supplanted Aryan power in Aryan lands. At best, we

---

[20] Several sub-narratives are sheltered under the foundational construct:

   i. Jews are good, thus things that are good for Jews are good: open societies, "democracy," mass immigration (into Europe/North America/Australia), destruction of (non-Jewish) families and traditional social norms, the intractable pursuit of money as an end and good, philanthropy aimed at non-Aryans, "equitable" governmental policies meant to quietly siphon resources from whites to non-whites, ignoring non-white crime in media and government policy, etc.

   ii. "Nazis" are evil: any species of (Aryan-centric) conservatism is threatening, "whites" are unhinged and dangerous/crimes committed by degenerate "whites" are highlighted in the media, European history is oppressive to non-whites, healthy lifestyles and traditional families are suspicious, etc.

   iii. Jews and the Holocaust cannot be questioned: discussion and debate on these topics — *if they are even legal* — are precluded because every attempt at either is met immediately with *ad hominem* attacks and non-sequiturs, if not outright violence.

Informationally, then, the stage is set for Jewish supremacy. Note: The current trend of Jew-obeisant media outlets and government officials openly questioning Israeli actions against Palestinians is both stratagem and destiny. As stratagem, it is the media-government attempt to appear balanced in their stance on the Jews — coming now after decades of both ignoring and enabling the issue and in a time of "rising anti-Semitism"; the media and governments are scrambling to appear legitimate, for *if Jews are criticized in the media and by government officials, how can the they be under Jewish control?* Conveniently for the Jews, none of this changes policy toward Israel or the Jewish Lobby, as Jewry will never be seriously criticized or questioned, the entertainment industry will continue to portray Jews as "heroic" and Aryans as evil/ignorant, aid will continue to flow to Israel and the Jewish Lobby, and political parties will do everything in their power to court all things Jewish. As destiny, it portends the Jewish urge to destruction: When Jews have parasitized non-Jews into oblivion, they will inevitably turn on each other and their destructive destiny will be fulfilled: "If the Jew ... were to triumph over the people of this world, his crown will be the funeral wreath of mankind. And this planet will once again follow its orbit through the

thus find in nearly every facet of life obsessive Jewish pushiness working to wedge apart Aryan families and communities. At worst, we see those who believe in the value of their race and the authority of those who defend it criminalized and demonized.

The vanity of the victors compels them, at every opportunity, to lord their material supremacy over Aryans, generally, and Hitlerists, specifically. We do not need to psychologically position ourselves in proximity to the absurdity of the offense — we *live* and *experience* the absurdly hate-filled vengeance and resentment of those who met the offense and rejected the faith it foreshadowed. The offense, for Hitlerists, is *palpable* and *immediate*. It is therefore Hitlerism that evokes "an awareness of how much must be lived and how difficult it is to become really aware of the difficulty of the decision."[21] Hitlerism — *faith in Adolf Hitler as manifestation of the Transcendent* — is sublime precisely because there are consequences to believing it; no doctrines can make such a sweeping boast, for historical doctrines are as invigorating as "thrusting a foot into the stocking."[22] The Hitlerist is fortunate to witness the Avatāra in his "true form and in the actual environment in which [he] didst walk here on earth; not in the form in which an empty and meaningless tradition, or a thoughtless and superstitious, or a gossipy historical tradition, has deformed Him."[23] And the Hitlerist is fortunate to experience the trials of the offense, for they reveal something of the Cosmic Struggle:

> If Adolf Hitler ... had physically won the war, Esoteric Hitlerism would not have been revealed ... [and] perhaps by now no space would exist for the *Avatar*, for having built an Anglo-Saxon-German Empire of the

---

ether devoid of humanity, just as it did millions of years ago" (Adolf Hitler, *Mein Kampf*).

[21] Kierkegaard, *Concluding Unscientific Postscript to Philosophical Fragments* vol. I (Princeton UP, 1992), translated by H. and E. Hong, 383.

[22] Kierkegaard, *Training in Christianity* (Vintage, 2004), 30. See, too, *Postscript*, 377: "Here again one sees the dubiousness of changing [faith] into a doctrine, where it is a matter of understanding..."

[23] Kierkegaard, *Training in Christianity* (Vintage, 2004), 5.

> White Race ... the entire Demiurgic and non-Demiurgic world would not have been included in a Holy War... [The physical victory of Adolf Hitler would have obfuscated] the discovery of the Enemy, the *robot* of the Enemy here on Earth: the International Jew.[24]

The unmasking of the Eternal Enemy has heightened the Cosmic Struggle to its final stage: The satanic war against the Hitlerian Idea was not merely a terrible material war; it was the *beginning of the end*, the *incarnation of the involution*, the *temporal instance of the Great Struggle between Good and Evil* — the outcome of which is the postwar offense that creates the conditions for the final victory of the Good. The Enemy is revealed and offense is taken — *for all time*. Tribulation is the sign and seal of divine pact; it is Nature's test of our loyalty:

> To such men as *concern me in any way* I wish suffering, desolation, sickness, ill treatment, indignities of all kinds. I wish them to be acquainted ... with the misery of the defeated: I have no pity for them; because I wish them to have the only thing which today proves whether a man has any value or not, namely, *the capacity of sticking to his guns*.[25]

Contemporaneousness with the offense and acceptance of the leap elevates the faithful Hitlerist to a level of authenticity and courageousness not seen for millennia. The first Hitlerists were coeval with the Führer; the greatest Hitlerists stayed loyal to the Führer even when the tide of the material struggle turned against the Reich, and the greatest among them stayed true even as the former Reich, and then the world, was rebuilt in Jehovah's image. Hitlerists today face a world full of enemies — hate-filled Judeo-enemies who seek the physical devastation of all traces of Adolf Hitler's legacy,

---

[24] Serrano, *Manu* (Hermitage Helm, 2017), 167.
[25] Nietzsche, *The Will to Power* (B&N, 2006), Book IV §910.

no matter the consequences. But this legacy will pass only when Nature itself ceases to exist, for *Hitler Avatāra is Nature.*

The Jewish propaganda machine, which roared to the fore of global affairs in the midst of two world wars, clears the way for the world's march toward Judeo-globalism: The Wandering Jew is only at home in a muddled, unnatural mix of peoples, for there it can hide in plain sight. From the first open calls to fight "the Huns"[26] and subsequent atrocity fictions to modernity's fabricated Judeo-definition of "race" and diabolical dreams of equality and equity, conventional propaganda continually announces the Jewish (and therefore the world's) view of the offense.

> When Jews step forward as the personification of in-nocence, the danger must be great.... the Jews: an in-stinctively crafty people, able to create an advantage, a means of *seduction* out of every conceivable hypothe-sis of superstition, even out of ignorance itself.[27]

But the Jews reveal themselves through their officiousness once again; they cannot stay hidden, no matter how hard they try: their parasitical behavior and absolute arrogance — i.e., their inescapable (demi)urge to follow their organic schema of *Jews + Nazis (Aryans) + Holocaust* — unmasks them. Jews have always followed their basic plot of acting in the best interests of Jews globally and against the interests of Gentiles — particularly Aryans, through destruction or enslavement — since their race began, since their manufacture in the mind of Jehovah. The advent of Adolf Hitler forever unmasked the Jew, however, because the Jew now openly admits its hatred of the Aryan and basks in the material victory the Jewish schema affords. Before Hitler Avatāra, Jewish power "hid" in victimization and internationalist creeds (e.g., Christianity, international

---

[26] From Mark C. Miller's introduction to Bernays' *Propaganda*: "The Anglo-American drive to demonize 'the Hun,' and to cast the war as a transcendent clash between Atlantic 'civilization' and Prussian 'barbarism,' made so powerful an impression on so many that the worlds of government and business were forever changed" (Ig Publishing, 2005, 12).

[27] *The Will to Power* (B&N, 2006), Book II §199.

socialism, Freemasonry, mercantilism, etc.); after Hitler Avatāra, Jews flaunt and sell victimization and internationalism to all — so that each individual imagines that these ideas come from his own mind and certainly haven't been planted there.[28] Jews are the embodiment of hate, which has its logical conclusion in destruction. Jewish offense, born out of resentment and vengeance, is permanent; but the Jewish victory, born out of their offense and catering, through Judeo-internationalist creeds, to the mass of filth populating this world, is temporary:

> The Communists will win; must win — for the time being — whether by force of arms or through the effect of their propaganda, it makes little difference. This is also natural — unavoidable. But this should not distress us. They — the exponents of the philosophy in accordance with the tendency of Time — will win, and pass: be annihilated by Time. We, the followers of [Adolf Hitler], "the Man against Time" ... will rise upon their ruins and rule, once more, a world, not of apes, but of regenerate, godlike men, Aryans in the full sense of the word.[29]

The offense of the Jews and the Judaized in the postwar world is the acceleration of time. Jewish pushiness is nudging the world ever more quickly toward its end. This Judeo-offense both made the Avatāra possible and was unmasked by the Avatāra, which is to say, the Avatāra completed the Judeo-offense; it is a paradox of thought which gives rise to the Paradox. "The one offended does not speak according to his own nature but according to the nature of the paradox..."[30] The Paradox dictates the outcome of the relationship between it and the offended; it is not the Jew who decides how it feels at the state of being that is Hitler Avatāra. And it is this Judeo-offense that makes contemporaneousness such a visceral and prox-

---

28 Bernays, *Propaganda* (Ig Publishing, 2005), 78.
29 Savitri Devi, *Gold in the Furnace* (1952), "Against Time."
30 Kierkegaard, *Philosophical Fragments* (Princeton UP, 1987), "Offense at the Paradox."

imate reality for the Hitlerist. But there is another side to the Hitlerist offense.

Savitri Devi spoke of the *lightning* and the *sun*; she lamented that Hitler's composition had "too much 'sun' and not enough 'lightning,'" which translated into traitorous and criminal elements being given the space to continue subverting Nature's Reich both domestically and abroad.

> From 1942 onwards, [Adolf Hitler] had ... faced and tackled the Jewish question ... with some amount of that ruthlessness with which it should have been tackled years before. But it was too late. That tardy mercilessness ... could no longer save the Reich. The mass-liquidation of about 750,000 Jews from Germany and other European countries ... did not prevent the influential Jews, living in safety [abroad] ... from directing the fury of all mankind, including that of the Aryan nations, against new Germany. (And after the war, when the fate of the few executed Jews ... became known in foreign lands, the figure of 750,000 became overnight 6,500,000 and even 8,000,000, in order to give the victorious Allies ... an excuse for torturing and killing as many of Adolf Hitler's followers as they could. While thousands of the most nefarious Jews had, thanks to the Führer's astounding generosity, already left Germany before the war.) ...
>
> And that, I repeat, because, contrarily to the Prophet Mohammed, contrarily to Lord Krishna, and to all Men "against Time" — both "Sun" and "Lightning" — who died victorious, our Führer had, in his personal makeup, too much sunshine in proportion to his "lightning" power.[31]

---

[31] Savitri Devi, *Lightning and the Sun* (Calcutta, 1958), 345-346. Revisionists put the number of persons — not merely Jews — exterminated during the so-called Holocaust at 570,000 (T. Dalton, *Debating the Holocaust* [Castle Hill, 2020], 260).

We lament that Hitler did not go far enough — that there was too much sun and not enough lightning to his nature. But this is the Hitlerist's vanity, for all happened precisely as was necessary for the fulfillment of Nature's course, as is recorded in all significant Indo-Aryan sacred texts: the cycle of time will bear its fated fruit. Hitler Avatāra unmasked the Jew for all time — this was his purpose; material victory for the Hitlerist has not yet ripened, though spiritual victory is assured; from Hitlerist Victory will come the New Order, the new time cycle, which will reestablish Nature's Order and make faith foregone.

Hitlerist faith, then, is predicated on the Judeo-offense that concretizes contemporaneousness with God and the Aryan offense that laments the divine mercy, which nonetheless created the conditions for our faith in a New Order. Hitlerist faith therefore *twice* meets the offense and marches onward — onward to the precipice that assures authenticity. Our leap is the morning that follows the darkest night; and while our faith ensures our survival, faith's purpose is the advent of an Order which does not need it. Thus the Paradox creates the paradox; thus time begins anew; thus we fight to create that which created us.

Have faith in and fight for your folk, *Kameraden. Gott mit uns.*

Heil Hitler!

— 6 —
Afterword

Exodus 40 and Numbers 7 describe a Jewish Black Mass consecrating the tabernacle for the Ark of the Covenant. Twelve elders in six covered wagons brought their offerings for the Demiurge-Jehovah: in all, 36 animals were slaughtered and burned for the "burnt offering"; 12 animals were slaughtered and burned for "purification"; 204 animals were slaughtered and burned for "well-being." In sum, 252 creatures were exsanguinated to satiate the Jehovahistic bloodlust. The Ark itself is symbolic of the Jewish anti-blood safeguarding the pact (covenant) Jews have with their god, Satan: provide blood sacrifices for Jehovah and bring Gentiles to ruin; for this, the Lord of Darkness will grant Jews lordship over the earth as the "Chosen Ones."

The exsanguination of living creatures for Jewish pleasure is called *kosher*.[1] In many parts of the West, *kosher* is synonymous with *proper*, *admissible*, *correct*, and *legitimate* — such is the pervasion of Jewish perversion in former Aryan lands.[2] One tries to imagine what a Jew must think when it bleeds living things dry for ritualistic satisfaction, but this is impossible — *the Jew is not human*, so non-Jewish minds cannot fathom their depravity.

> The [Jews] are programmed to give to Jehovah periodic and bloody sacrifices of human beings, and preferably of semi-divine *Vîras*. In return, Jehovah transfers an energy to them that is not human but from an infra-human Universe. But this is not enough for the [Jew-machine] to work. Jehovah must have the food of human blood in the same way as it needs the creative genius of the Aryan ... to maintain and perfect his dwell-

---

[1] From the Hebrew *kāšēr*.
[2] We leave the "kosher" tax on foodstuffs, indicated by any number of "kosher" symbols in pantries across the globe, for another time.

ing on Earth.... The story of Dracula shows us the most hidden reality of those non-human beings. *Dracula* is the autobiography of the [Jew]. For his vampire survival he must suck Aryan and non-Aryan blood, thus prolonging indefinitely its Zombie existence while absorbing the magic substance.[3]

This is wholly unimaginable, yet it *is* here. Bizarre occurrences are commonplace today, though they are nonetheless bizarre. The Judaized world guarantees a type of perpetual ordered chaos — a consecrated mix of just enough societal instability to keep non-Jews bemused but consuming and just enough stability to set conditions for increases in Jewish power. This is the purpose of the Ark, after all. For all the bizarreness that dominates modernity, however, the case of the Jew remains inconceivable — not because its actions over millennia have not proven its nefariousness, but because the healthy Aryan mind simply cannot imagine the absolute evil of a vampire — not to write a story about such a thing, but to actually perceive the world and act in such parasitical a way. It is unimaginable to lie about, obfuscate, or circumambulate *everything* — but this is just what the Jew, the Organic Lie, does. Fear not, however: Jewry's existence in this time cycle is necessary — necessary and fleeting.

∞ ∞ ∞

The ultimate heroes of this time must be grateful to the Führer, because He upheld so great a war, so enormous a combat, such heroic sacrifice, in the fulfillment of an Eternal Symbol, making possible for new generations to give themselves to Him and in Him to meet a Destiny, a salvation, an Ideal, a Myth of Redemption. So as we have seen and *understood*, we already know a God was again among men, together with the heroes; the true God of heroes, not the god of

---

[3] Serrano, *Manu* (Hermitage Helm, 2017), 179-180; translation modified for readability.

> slaves; the God of Brahmins, of the Hyperborean Hosts, God of the Aryans, not the god of Jews. And the new religion that will manifest itself, the new Myth that is fulfilled, is the ancient Polar Myth, when Gods inhabited the Earth and lived among heroes.[4]

Heroes populate our world, our time. Though they are the minority, these are men and women of quality, authentic quality that cannot be conquered. These are loyal and honorable folk who value and therefore fight for their kin, clan, and blood — this is what makes them heroic. The future belongs to he who holds the last hope, to she who remains faithful in the struggle. The healthy and strong Aryans will endure and outlast the diseased and degenerate masses, so do not let fear conquer your faith. Our folk created all that is good in this world; and our folk will reestablish the good that's been lost after the Judaized masses have had their reign. We look to the Führer, *our* Führer as the bastion of the Good; all of Nature will fill our ranks when we uphold the Hitlerian Idea. And we remain pure in heart — we remember that *purity of heart is to will one thing.*

Hitler Avatāra did not walk among us as an *historical being* — as long as one of us continues the struggle we *are* Hitler Avatāra; this is not to say that we are God, but only that we commune with God. Adolf Hitler is an archetype, a symbol, the Aryan will incarnate. When we embody his tenets, we celebrate his life; we find that his life and its ensuing consequences are equally essential and essentially equal. When we embody his tenets, we *are* the offense, and we are thus the faith necessary to bring about a New Aryan Order.

Let love ignite actions that will concretize the divine revolution. And remember that *what is done out of love always takes place beyond good and evil.* Love does what is necessary. Nature is necessary; Nature is harmony; Nature is vengeance; Nature is ours. The future is lit by the fire of necessity.

---

[4] Serrano, *Adolf Hitler: The Ultimate Avatar* (Hermitage Helm, 2014), 178.

When this earth has passed, "Only the Resurrected Heroes shall remain, beyond the stars..."[5] — this is the light of the Black Sun, emergent and concealed, projecting and revealing itself, loyally lighting the dark across time for those who once again take up the struggle, the paradox of the Paradox: *The light beyond the stars — the morning of a day that has ended, the morning of a day that has yet to come; it is the light from the eyes of those born with eyes open. It is the light that reaches us nonetheless.*

> The objective of our struggle is well known. It is none other than to preserve the existence of our folk, which God has created.... It is our duty to remain steadfast before Him, so that we shall be accorded the merciful judgment which calls itself "victory" and means life.
>
> — Adolf Hitler

---

[5] Serrano, *Manu* (Hermitage Helm, 2017), 286.

— 7 —
Rebellion

If the possessor of power abuses his authority, if he does not fulfill the obligations which men have always considered inseparable from power, the victims of such abuse are entitled to consider themselves released from their own obligations.

— Peter Hoffmann,
The History of the German Resistance

Eighty years after the fall of the Germanic world and the overt ascent of the Jewish one, governments across the West are ignoring, denouncing, or, more often, actively supporting the agitators within their own countries. Government action is predicated on agitator orientation within the left-right political construct. As the West hurtles toward sanctioned (and authoritarian) leftism, sanctioned agitation is *always* leftist and, if progressive causes are not adopted today, it is certain that we take progressive steps toward their adoption tomorrow. *Leftism*, as Kaczynski incisively describes, is the totalitarian and authoritarian ideology *par excellence*; it is worth quoting him at length here so we might plainly see our enemy:

> The leftist is anti-individualistic, pro-collectivist. He wants society to solve everyone's problems for them, satisfy everyone's needs for them, take care of them. He is not the sort of person who has an inner sense of confidence in his ability to solve his own problems and satisfy his own needs. The leftist is antagonistic to the concept of competition because, deep inside, he feels like a loser.... His feelings of inferiority are so ingrained that he cannot conceive of himself as individually strong and valuable.... He can feel strong only as a

member of a large organization or a mass movement with which he identifies himself....

Leftists protest by lying down in front of vehicles, they intentionally provoke [abuse]. These tactics may often be effective, but many leftists use them not as a means to an end but because they *prefer* masochistic tactics. Self-hatred is a leftist trait.... The decisive role played by feelings of inferiority, low self-esteem, powerlessness, [and] identification with victims by people who are not themselves victims, is a peculiarity of modern leftism....

But no matter how far the movement has gone in attaining its goals the leftist is never satisfied, because his activism is a surrogate activity. That is, the leftist's real motive is not to attain the ostensible goals of leftism; in reality he is motivated by the sense of power he gets from struggling for and then reaching a social goal. Consequently the leftist is never satisfied with the goals he has already attained; his need for the power process leads him always to pursue some new goal.[1]

The anti-individualistic inferiority and obsessive need to control every aspect of life and society is quintessentially Jewish, and it manifests as "resentment, popular insurrection, the revolt of the bungled and the botched."[2] That *every leftist organization in history* has had at least a clique of Jews integral to its composition and/or inspiration, then, should come as no surprise. The West's rapid leftist drift[3] exists

---

[1] *Industrial Society and Its Future*, paragraphs 16, 19, 20, 219, and 232.
[2] Friedrich Nietzsche, *The Will to Power* (B&N, 2006), translated by Anthony Ludovici, §90.
[3] America is arguably the most "conservative" of all Western countries, and it has been descending rapidly into the progressive abyss since the early twentieth century, if not the mid-nineteenth century. The Pew Research Center has charted the more recent leftward shift in American political views (1994-2017, "The Shift in the American Public's Political Values"); see also *The New York Times'* "Young Voters Keep Moving to the Left on Social Issues, Republicans Included" (2019), *The American*

because its institutions are occupied by Jews and their agents. However, the entire left-right paradigm, in a Jewish World Order, is false: there are only Jewish (and non-Jewish) interests.[4] Left or right, Jewish interests are being catered to across the West:

- Mass immigration of non-European peoples into European lands;
- Constant conflict and war profiteering;
- Incessant praise and aid to Israel or complicit ignorance of Jewish actions in the Middle East;
- Constant "reminder" of the Holocaust;[5]
- Exploitative capitalism;
- Overemphasis on distracting entertainment;
- Degenerate and sensational media-educational systems designed to indoctrinate and traumatize the citizenry;
- The rule of money (as opposed to the "rule of law" that is so often mentioned);
- Technocrats and governmental yes-men spouting Jewish slogans to win public support for harmful policies (and maintain their sources of income), etc.

Prospect's "Most Americans Are Liberal, Even If They Don't Know It" (2017), and *The Atlantic*'s "Why America is Moving Left" (2016) for a sampling of the topic.

[4] This is not to say that *left* and *right* do not exist in the Judeo-system, but only that regardless of where one sits on the "liberal-democratic" spectrum, one is advocating for Jewish interests. There are "left-wing" Jews and "right-wing" Jews (not to mention allies), but all are subordinate to the eternal Jewish law: Jewish supremacy and Aryan destruction/enslavement. When the non-Jews are finally gone (physically or mentally), the Jews will turn on each other, thus completing their spiteful, destructive arc. Hitler, after all, wanted to send all European Jews to Madagascar — because he knew they would eventually destroy themselves if left to their own devices (i.e., if left without a host).

[5] Irmin Vinson's *Some Thoughts on Hitler and Other Essays* evenly and astutely discusses the reasons for the West's obsession with the Holocaust.

All of these interests feed the principal Jewish aim of destabilization, which, in turn, has its aim of breaking and conquering host
populations to enable Jewish supremacy. The Jews will not stop
until their host is enslaved or extinct, as has been their practice for
millennia.[6]

We are a people under duress. We are a people under attack.
Knowing agents within our governments, media, and academia
have *already* conspired against us for personal profit; this is why
loathsome agendas are pushed and enforced without regard for
popular support.[7] A society under leftist control would, in fact, look
like what most Western societies look like today with:

- "Hate speech" and "hate crime" laws;
- Controlled and censored publishing;
- Compelled speech;

---

[6] See the following works (list not exhaustive): *Classic Essays on the Jewish Question* and *Eternal Strangers* (Thomas Dalton); *Myth of the Twentieth Century* and *The Track of the Jew through the Ages* (Alfred Rosenberg); *The Jewish Strategy* (Revilo Oliver); *You Gentiles* (Maurice Samuel); *The Biological Jew* (Eustace Mullins); *The International Jew* (Henry
Ford); *The Riddle of the Jews' Success* (Theodor Fritsch); *The Jews and
Modern Capitalism* (Werner Sombart); *Capitalism and the Jews* (Jerry
Muller).

[7] We see the oligarchs and technocrats routinely and openly discuss their
plans for the future — at Davos, the World Economic Forum, the Sun
Valley Conference, Jackson Hole, Bilderberg, Bohemian Grove,
DealBook, etc. Larry Fink, the Jewish CEO of BlackRock, can unabashed-
ly say at a DealBook conference (2017) that leftist agendas must be
"forced" upon the people: "You have to force behaviors ... If you don't
force behaviors, ... you're going to be [financially] impacted.... We're going to have to force change." Thus we have company after company
proudly showcasing this or that perverse agenda. Invariably, the perverse
narrative stems from the company's majority shareholders (usually
BlackRock, Vanguard, or State Street). And, nearly as invariably, Jews
have prominent roles with the majority shareholders. More importantly,
however, is the undeniable fact that *perverted people push perversion.*
The millionaire and billionaire "elites" supporting perversion *are* perverted — if they were not, they wouldn't care so deeply about normaliz-
ing deviance.

- Selective education (i.e., exposure to some ideas as opposed to others, which facilitates mass ignorance and/or deviance);
- Compulsory communities (forced racial and ideological integration);
- The glamorization of perversion and debasement of honorable, traditionalist values;
- Forced emplacement of so-called minorities in positions of authority (or the forced reallocation of resources to enable this), etc.

A leftist's dream, then, is not a society that's much different conceptually and structurally than what we find today (perhaps the ideal is just *more* of what already is); the one glaring deficiency is the residual existence of dissenters. Fulfillment of the leftist's dream, then, would entail one further extreme: those who dissent from the progressive worldview — the prevailing view today — must *vanish*; they must be purged once and for all. At the moment, the Leftist West tries to rid itself of dissenters through "legal" means and overwhelming propaganda. Eventually, however, all pretenses to "legality" will evaporate and leftist states will openly target, transfer, and terminate dissenters. This is the future that both is and waits. And if society is plodding ever so willingly in the desired direction of its Jewish masters, the time for action is all the more urgent; for the willing are freely in bondage, and what remains is a society of masters and lapdogs — not freedom. This is the seed of revolution.

What follows describes what has happened, what is happening, and what will happen as a result of oppression within the false left-right paradigm; it describes methods used by both friend and foe. As Hitlerists, we stand above the Jewish construct of *left* and *right* — our guide is always Nature.[8] The Jewish paradigm can only

---

[8] *Nature* represents "those aspects of the functioning of the Earth and its living things that are independent of human management and free of human interference and control. And with wild Nature we include human nature, by which we mean those aspects of the functioning of the human individual that are not subject to regu-

be destroyed from within, both individually and collectively. Whether this destruction comes via the inevitable Jewish global war (ritual sacrifice) or through the efforts of fifth columnists remains to be seen and is largely immaterial. Our first task is to cleanse our thinking of Jewish influence, a guide for which is offered in the preceding pages; when this is done, the war is already won, for we will have the righteous cause of liberation branded on our being.

Adolf Hitler will not appeal to many people in the current Jewish World Order, as they have been fed lies or half-truths for decades. Adolf Hitler is not the Hitlerist's goal, however; Nature is. The Hitlerist must therefore appeal to the fundamental goodness and rightness of Nature as the binding, central feature of any New Order. A focus on Nature and noncontroversial commonalities, along with simply highlighting the rampant sociopolitical corruption plaguing the West, will be sufficient to increase public support for material rebellion.[9] The Hitlerist, then, as one who undertakes the

---

lation by organized society but are products of chance, or free will, or God" (Kaczynski, *ISAIF*, paragraph 183).

[9] In addition to corruption, we appraise the technocrats and techno-priests, salivating at the prospect of an increasingly dumbed-down "proletariat" of the future. The influential Jew Yuval Harari, in his book *Homo Deus* (HarperCollins, 2017), likes to imagine man as God, creating a "technological bonanza" that will render most people "useless" — they "will not merely be unemployed ... [but] unemployable." What to do with such people until they can be very *democratically* removed from society? Simply keep them "occupied ... [with] drugs and computer games." Jews are wont to dictate their *liberal-democratic* terms to the masses, and the best magicians are able to trick the mind with distractions and subtlety. Nature is much more frightening to Jews than man, which is why Jews are both so eager to "force," as Larry Fink would say, a world into existence that suits Jewry's man-centered interests, and so keen to vilify Nature and those who uphold it. Harari's flippancy in suggesting the salve of "drugs and ... games" to sooth the masses is repellent because he knows it's Jews who are pulling the strings. Jewish hands will guide the demise of the masses; and these same Jewish hands will stuff their pockets with whatever ill-gotten gains they can wring from the ragged people. The Jews' very existence is pretext for fleecing.

daily struggle of individual revolution, is the spiritual heart of a broader struggle against time, against the Judeo-material forces leading the world to thralldom and devastation.

The Organized Rebellion

Organized rebellions are comprised of irregular (i.e., not state-sponsored) forces that aim to control territory within the country they operate — whether the entire country via revolution, or a portion of the country via separatism. Organized rebellions are distinguished from terrorist organizations by their ultimate aim, as terrorist organizations often have goals apart from garnering territory. *Terrorism*, however, is often a tactic of insurgencies. Mystic cults, having supra-territorial ambitions, are not typically considered rebellions, but perhaps *accelerants* to a desired utopia. However, such cults might also be leveraged to achieve more worldly aims; these groups might not be wholly manageable, so care must be taken if collaborating. Criminal syndicates, too, which operate for the sake of their criminal enterprise, are not rebellions; if proper rebellions lose their spiritual-ideological anchor, they can and have devolved into mere criminal gangs.[10] Regardless of one's identity — as rebel, terrorist, applied mystic, or criminal — the following methods broadly capture the nature and structure of oppositional organizations. All such organizations, excepting the criminal-for-criminality's-sake enterprises (e.g., gangs), for the purposes of this discussion, will be considered *rebellions*.

Rebellions are comprised of guerrillas, an underground, and an auxiliary network — the purpose of which is to strike where the state least expects it and is most vulnerable. While guerrillas are the visible part of a rebellion, the underground and auxiliary are the invisible elements providing coordinated capabilities for the rebellion.

---

[10] Notably, criminal gangs are dear to the leftist regime because (1) they lend themselves to societal destabilization and (2) they are disproportionately and overwhelmingly comprised of non-Aryans, which feeds the leftist victimization trope and the leftist need to identify with the "other" victim. It is no surprise, then, that many modern leftist regimes in the West promote "gangster" or "thug" culture; it's also no surprise that the media-entertainment industry glorifying such culture is largely Jewish.

Undergrounders often make up the core of a rebellion and are considered the "professionals" of the lot. Most, if not all, of their time and effort are dedicated to the movement and its needs. They might assume a false identity and tend to be less involved in their surrounding community. Auxiliary members, on the other hand, will lead a "double life," living as ordinary members of their community while providing occasional support to the movement. When state suspicion burdens the auxiliary member, he will often abandon his community life and move to the underground or the guerrilla force.

As the main support section of the movement, the auxiliary is the essential coordinating and organizational node. Anyone belonging to the auxiliary must be disciplined and inconspicuous. Without the auxiliary, neither the guerrillas nor the underground can hope to endure, so it is critical the auxiliary members be competent. In addition to indispensable logistical support, the auxiliary also provides vital intelligence for the movement. Notably, auxiliary and underground functions often overlap; but auxiliaries are expected to be the necessary link to the communities in which the rebellion operates.

External Assistance

If a rebellion becomes significant enough — both in capability and duration — it will attract foreign aid. Aid can come in myriad forms, from money and arms to intelligence, training, and harbor. Support could be motivated by the desire for influence, retribution, regime change, prestige, ideological support, or simply the hope to plunder what remains after the struggle. The rebel will have to weigh the costs associated with the likely needed external aid.

Foreign aid has often been the deciding factor in conflict — whether conventional or unconventional. American support to the Soviets played a significant role in the outcome of World War II; Soviet support to the Viet Cong, along with a more focused strategy and will, helped determine Viet Nam's fate; French support to the Americans during the revolution was critical in helping the upstarts defeat an empire.

Despite the importance of foreign support, however, it is not the sole determining factor. One must consider, above all, the will to win, discipline, and morale, along with superior strategy and organization.[11] If these things are lacking, materiel support is a moot point. Nevertheless, aid can be beneficial. One must assess the interests of the foreign power providing help, and decide if the help will be mutually advantageous or simply one-sided.

Other means — coercive (e.g., intimidation) and non-coercive (e.g., cooperation or appropriation) — may also be used to generate funds and supplies. These, particularly cooperation, are often the lifeblood of rebellions.

The Guerrilla War

Mao Zedong was right in his reflection that rebellions must have both political purpose and popular support if they are to succeed. "We advance our aim of destroying the enemy by propagandizing his troops, by treating his captured soldiers with dignity, and by treating those of his wounded who fall into our hands. If we fail on these points, we strengthen the enemy's solidarity." Mao led one of the most successful rebellions in history; this was no accident, so perhaps there are lessons to be learned.

It is true that the war between National Socialism and the Judeo-Allies was existential; caring for the enemy's troops was an afterthought. But this was a total war, not a rebellion. Certainly, the uncompromising actions of all sides birthed partisans behind the frontlines, but such action was necessary: Providence willed it because Hitler and Judeo-Allied leaders willed it. In modern times, when ideologies hide themselves behind ideologies, or at least abstractions, the methods of past successful rebellions might again prove fruitful. Time will tell.

Mao instructs his listeners to "withdraw, deliver a lightning blow, seek a lightning decision."[12] This is a *Blitzkrieg* for a different world, for a world in which the good must exercise patience. We

---

[11] Jeffery Record, "External Assistance: Enabler of Insurgent Success," *Parameters* (Autumn 2006), 36-48.

[12] Mao Zedong, "Primer on Guerrilla War."

also acknowledge the turning point of the Eastern Front, when the Soviet Army became the influence for Mao's own later tactics, as the Reich's Army "won itself to death" or "punched into air": *the [guerrilla] formula in sixteen words: enemy advances, we retreat; enemy halts, we harass; enemy tires, we attack; enemy retreats, we pursue.* Guerrilla tactics have benefited every outgunned force of historical note.

Home is where the rebel lays his head. The front is where he engages the enemy. No matter the setting, no matter the representative of the enemy — animate or inanimate — the rebel strikes and disperses. Disciplined initiative is the essence of the guerrilla and the rebellion. One must be disciplined to keep the ultimate goal always in mind, and one must have the vigor to act both when problems and opportunities arise: "the urban guerrilla cannot let himself become confused, or wait for orders. His duty is to act, to find adequate solutions for each problem he faces, and not to retreat. It is better to err acting than to do nothing for fear of erring. Without initiative there is no ... guerrilla warfare."[13]

In the early stages of an armed rebellion against a modern state, infrastructure is the underbelly. Subvert it and you disrupt the state-sponsored Nature-subverters. Infrastructure involves food, energy, equipment, ammunition, communication, and transportation — these resources are important for friend and foe, so one must carefully observe and manage them. The rebel sets his sights on infrastructure and watches the veneer peel away from the rotted walls of society. Raids, ambushes, harassments, *selections* of valued marks — these are the foci of the rebel. Destabilize the *state*; extend and unravel its supply and communication lines; further erode the people's trust in a corrupt state.

An important distinction on *destabilization* must be made: A rebellion for the cause of restoring the preeminence of Nature seeks the destabilization of the *state* to destroy the state; the Judeo-state seeks the destabilization of *society* to destroy the individual. For the rebellion, people are the goal, not territory; people need

---

[13] Carlos Marighella, *Mini-Manual of the Urban Guerrilla* (Guillen Press, 2002), 5.

food, water, clothing, shelter, and security — if the state cannot provide these, the sate has failed. Which of these can the rebellion disrupt? Which of these can it provide? Whatever the answer, the rebel chooses his objectives with consideration. It is true that a rebellion is outgunned by the state-sponsored forces; but the rebellion will likely have the support of the oppressed people behind it; any future rebellion must have the impetus of Nature behind it. This moral superiority gives the revolutionary movement a decided advantage, and this is what sustains it. The Nature-bound, revolutionary verve is what drives the movement to achieve its principal duty: attack, survive, and reorient.

The rebel preserves his forces by hitting sure high-value marks and immediately disengaging. "Our strategy is one against ten and our tactics are ten against one," as Mao said.[14] When the rebel falls back, he "moves among the people like a fish moves through the water" — or he perhaps has some remote, rugged terrain at which he's based. He moves in small units of perhaps three or four, and rarely in groups of more than nine; speed and mobility are his security. Fall back and buy time, build support, gain momentum.

The rebel arises from underground; he is at home in the nondescript, for only the ordinary can hope to elude the prying eyes of the modern state. The underground is the base of the rebellion. When the rebellion's fighters — the guerrillas — fall for the cause, the underground remains strong; martyrs for the cause are more evidence of the state's tyrannical oppression.[15] Small cells in every community characterize the underground. The size of the cells remains steady, but the number of cells grows. Each state-sponsored crackdown is more fuel for the fire. The tyrannical state can only hate and oppress; money and power are its masters, not people.

---

[14] *The Selected Works of Mao Tse-tung*, "Problems of China's Revolutionary War" (Lawrence & Wishart, 1964).

[15] Certain agitators have used women and children for demonstrative acts to embarrass the police or stifle their reaction. Some groups have also used women and children to mock state-sponsored forces to provoke an attack; any attack against women or children would, naturally, ignite the population's rage. One must always act in accordance with one's values.

Where one *undergrounder* falls, two more are created. Remind the people of their servitude; if, after reminding, they do not care, the soft underbelly of infrastructure is there to reorient them. And remind the people of why the state fears their noncompliance: The state is corrupt, serving only injustice and perversion — people are everywhere subjugated and lulled gradually into servitude; representatives of the state are despotic and flout Nature, imposing whatever creed brings them more status and money, and each presumes the state, and therefore *they*, are god; the state fears the people because the state knows it exists on borrowed time.

If the movement is to go anywhere, it must grow beyond conspiracy and into the realm of mass support. Indiscriminate admittance into the rebellion must be avoided, however. Internal security must be paramount. The rebellion will eventually be infiltrated, but mitigate this by implementing rigorous screening processes, lengthy probationary periods, loyalty checks, and pitiless responses to spies. An undergrounder perhaps introduces potential partisans to the idea of a political discussion group — and the relationship develops from there. Loyalty checks can be used to ensure fidelity: oaths can be *written* and *signed*; questionnaires, which capture as much personal data as necessary, might be devised to explore a prospect's position on any number of topics important to the movement; monitored engagements might be arranged to test the prospect's mettle. Screening and probationary periods might last two years or more; the successful rebel is a patient one.

An effective rebellion keeps a loosely controlled network of roughly autonomous cells, each not knowing more than what is absolutely necessary for their individual function; the mortar is the ideologically minded cadre keeping the cells focused and active. The ideology is Nature; therefore control does not fall with any one man. Network leaders are agreed upon locally and appointed through a central commission. Leadership may be decided locally until consensus cannot be reached; then, central leadership can resolve any lack of consensus. Organizational culture will decide general movement rules of engagement — whether these are set locally or centrally; some central oversight might be best, but more radical elements have fostered a more decentralized approach.

Leaders must determine the trajectory of their movement by striking a balance between operational and informational successes and deliberate recruiting. Ultimately, growth opportunities must be seized and successes must be followed with planned successive engagement — but the security costs of growing too quickly must be weighed. Whatever its size, the network must extend across the largest possible area and appeal to the greatest number of sympathizers; this will offer the chance for the broadest impact and will further thin state-sponsored forces. In extending invitations to various partisans, *individual character* must never be compromised. If a rebellion is solely comprised of one type of people, it will be easy prey for the state; successful rebellions have always cast discriminating but wide nets.

Effective rebellions have also brought skilled professionals into the fold. If one imagines all the necessary tasks to realize the goal of destroying deviance, exorcising corruption, and toppling tyranny, one can easily see how medical personnel, farmers, food distributors, police, mechanics, electricians, welders, printers, postal workers, drivers, carpenters, soldiers, chemists, and machinists would be valuable assets. A rebellion must avoid, however, sympathizers likely under surveillance; obvious targets of the state would include the biggest influencers, leaders, and teachers in their various fields. Just as prominent social-media influencers now are targeted by the state to push sanctioned messages to mass audiences, prominent sympathizers of the rebellion would be prime targets for the state under more serious conditions. The state is devious, but it is not infallible and all-powerful. The rebel recalls Mao: *Our strategy is one against ten and our tactics are ten against one.* The successful rebel is deliberate, thoughtful.

Moreover, the effective partisan is modest and composed, dependable and sober, reserved and watchful: He protects his goals by having them ever in mind. Boasting is for the state and its thoughtless lapdogs. All this must be part of the rebellion's enculturation process. When cell members meet, they meet in places where suspicion is avoided, where the comings and goings of people will go unnoticed: an isolated wood, a bustling park or square, a neutral establishment. Perhaps they choose to meet on holidays, birthdays, or anniversaries as pretext for gathering. Whatever the case, the rebel changes his routine frequently; he does not follow a pattern. Even initially innocuous activities might draw notice if they are oft repeated. The effective rebel considers every detail of a meeting: Should arrivals and departures be staggered? Should trusted family members be present to deflect suspicion? Should a trail party be designated for clearing any damning evidence? Rebellions do all they can to prevent detectable routine.

A rebellion aims to avoid capture, but prepares members for its possibility. The state will use all means of coercion at its disposal to turn rebels into informants: it will lie, torture, trick, and even befriend to get information from the captive; do not be duped by the agent provocateur, or the "cellmate," or the "awed" official wondering about "clever" methods or promising amnesty. The captured rebel gives up nothing and no one. Know that the state will slander the compromised individual or cell in an attempt to deflect attention from its (i.e., the state's) wrongdoing.[16] In a 2001 press release, the Earth Liberation Front (ELF) observed that "labeling the ELF as *violent* ... is a means by which mainstream society, government, and big business can attempt to forget about the real true violence which occurs [every day], the violence against life." The state is the terrorizer, the tyrant, and the embodiment of evil — any deal it offers is tainted, so it must not be accepted. If an undergrounder is released from state internment, he must be observed to determine if reintegration is possible.

---

[16] In his definitive *Yockey* (Arktos, 2018), Kerry Bolton catalogues just a few of the many cases where the traditionalist is not merely slandered, but *pathologized* — incarcerated, if not erased altogether. Among this libeled lot are such luminaries as Ezra Pound, Knut Hamsun, and Yockey himself. Bolton cites the Jew Adorno's *The Authoritarian Personality* (1950), funded by the American Jewish Committee, as "[diagnosing] traditional conservative values such as respect for parents as a symptom of mental illness, along with any signs of (white) loyalty to one's own race or negative thoughts about Jews. The family per se is regarded as the seedbed of 'Fascism'." (Bolton, 370n38)

Propaganda

As popular support is essential for any rebellion, it is important to send the messages that will most effectively win that support.[17] Effective messages must: (1) be tailored to specific audiences (messages without a specific audience are largely ineffective; at the very least, it will be difficult to gauge the effectiveness of messages with unspecific audiences); (2) affect an audience's existing attitudes rather than try to completely change an attitude; (3) be believable; (4) eventually, if not immediately, ask for audience action — this is best done by tying the sought-after change to the audience's well-being.

Messaging can come via traditional information channels, or it might come in the form of a physical action (with intended psychological effect). Regardless of the means of conveyance, the message must be well considered. Because most messaging will occur via traditional information channels, propagandizing responsibility will typically fall to the underground (with guerrillas providing certain psychological actions or acting as means of dissemination in some cases). It is crucial, then, that the underground use the best means of communication available to the intended audience.

Typical audiences include: (1) the enemy, with agitation, confusion, and damaging their morale as goals; (2) enemy sympathizers, with the aim of winning their support; (3) the neutral population, with the goal of either galvanizing their support or, at least, dissuading them from supporting the enemy; (4) friendly sympathizers, to provide motivation, unity, and calls to action; (5) foreign

---

[17] Recent "failed" messaging from major retailers (e.g., Target, Anheuser-Busch) pushing degenerate agendas resulted in a boycotting backlash; this situation arose because the company decision-makers and propagandists failed to look at how certain messages would land outside of their immediate, perverted circles. Unfortunately, these messages only ostensibly "failed" because the average consumer is ignorant and apathetic enough to let the companies get away with their attempts to corrupt the population. This, of course, is precisely why the West is in the state it's in now — ignorance and apathy. There is no reason to assume it will change because of a few aberrant messages.

supporters, with the objective of winning financial or material help and international (diplomatic) recognition.

Carlos Marighella describes a "war of nerves" that must be waged against a tyrannical state:

- Use the telephone and the mail to announce false clues to the police and the government, including information on the planting of bombs and other acts of terrorism in public offices and other places, kidnaping and assassination plans, etc., to oblige the authorities to wear themselves out, following up on the information fed them;
- Let false plans fall into the hands of the police to divert their attention;
- Plant rumors to make the government uneasy;
- Exploit by every means possible the corruption, the errors, and failures of the government and its representatives, forcing them into demoralizing explanations and justifications in the very mass communication media they maintain under censorship;
- Present denunciations to foreign embassies, the United Nations, the papal nunciature, and the international judicial commissions defending human rights or freedom of the press, exposing each concrete violation and use of violence by the military dictatorship and making it known that the revolutionary war will continue its course with serious danger for the enemies of the people.[18]

The war of nerves, as indicated, is meant to further disperse and disturb the efforts of state-sponsored forces, which, naturally, is part of every revolutionary movement. Openly question the state and people will lose confidence in its institutions; make the state

---

[18] Marighella, *Mini-Manual of the Urban Guerrilla* (A. Guillen Press, 2002), 31.

question itself and confidence melts like ice under salt — i.e., the conditions will then be set for further action.

Reflections
As we close this discussion of what's worked in prior rebellions (and what perhaps might work again), I would like to make two clarifying remarks.

First, what I have presented here is not novel. I do not claim to have come up with much of this on my own. This is a broad distillation of thoughts and practices reaching back several decades, with even these being products of still older rebellious experiences. I encourage the reader to research the topic for himself, reading even deeper into the matter, learning specifics about the general ideas presented here, and using sound judgment on how and where to research.

Second, I would like to say what this study is not. Bard O'Neill identifies five types of revolutionary movement rationales:

1. *Pluralist* — seeks to destroy or displace the existing system in favor of individual freedom and liberty.
2. *Egalitarian* — seeks to destroy the existing system to impose one founded on equal distribution of social and/or physical goods.
3. *Traditionalist* — seeks to replace a given system with one based on the application of *primordial* and *sacred values*, often rooted in ancestral or religious lineage.
4. *Anarchist* — strives for the permanent destruction of a given institutionalized system, discarding all authority patterns as illegitimate and unnecessary.
5. *Apocalyptic-Utopian* — seeks to destroy the current order in preparation for an apocalypse.[19]

---

[19] *Insurgency & Terrorism: From Revolution to Apocalypse* (Potomac Books, 2005), 20-24.

A pluralist rebellion is out of the question. Access to individual freedom and liberty presumes a certain amount of individual intelligence, which, frankly, most people do not have. Moreover, a pluralist rebellion assumes what we cannot: that most people are decent and thinking. It also assumes that the current system has not utterly corrupted both itself and its participants, which we also cannot assume. Ultimately, the pluralist must imagine, *If only the system were shed, we'd be much better off...* We must take this further and say, *Yes, the system must be shed, but also a great many people.*

Who decides who stays and goes? Well, many educated folks have tried to answer this question since civilization began — yet here we are; I'm inclined to believe that education has made more than a few dignitaries more than a little dull. Perhaps we would do well to reclaim some of our past "barbarousness" and start by ridding ourselves of the metastasized notion that all humans, simply because they are human, have *inherent dignity*. This absurd belief has no foundation outside Judeo-Christianity and has done more harm to Aryan folk than anything else — by Judeo-design, no doubt. *Might makes right* is the unbending truth of history. The unthinking quantity has supposed this to mean "we the people," and that the "strength in numbers" majority is right. If anything good remains of humanity and if we are to have any meaningful future, this truth must be reclaimed for the *quality* among us — *the might of quality makes right*. Once — or *if* — this is figured out, the answer to who stays and who goes is quite clear.

It is apparent, then, that the egalitarian and anarchist rebellions are likewise incomprehensible. These rebellions are utterly Jewish and pave the way for Jewish supremacy. If one is curious about what the post-egalitarian-rebellion world would look like, simply turn on the news or walk down the street — a revolt of the *bungled* and the *botched* indeed! As for the anarchist, he is simply a Nihilist. What good is he and what good does he bring to others? The artless anarchist has evidently never lived among those who strive for his demise; he is nothing more than Jewry's tool.

The traditionalist and apocalyptic rebellions remain. It is certainly true that any creed espousing Nature as the utmost lawgiver and arbiter would, in due course, evoke primordial and sacred values. Hitlerists adhere to Nature, and whether Hitlerism dies on the vine or not, *Nature will win out.* Is there a difference between the traditionalist who seeks to invoke primordial values and the apocalyptarian working toward the end? No — the end will come regardless of method.

Perhaps revolution will never happen again in America, or in the West, generally; perhaps it's too far gone, too tightly ensnared in the liberal trap. Despite alleged "left" and "right" dichotomies, all march to the same Jewish tune, the same drumbeat of money-distraction. Too few people are racially aware. Good breeding makes good sense for animals — but not for humans. Of course! It would be *racist* to think otherwise! More detrimental to any salvific cause is White ignorance. Far too many Whites fall for liberal tricks. It's not *only* the despicable Whites, for instance, who take roles in media programming that suggests miscegenation; it's not *only* the despicable Whites who fail to see the trick for what it is and find the unnatural normal; it's not *only* the despicable White politicians and businesspersons who push their perverted agendas for the sake of money — no, *it's all of them together.* They coalesce to form an inescapable abyss.

Whatever remaining *normal* — i.e., not odious, not ignorant — values-based, traditionalist families there are, their only salvation is collapse. And collapse our current system will. It will not readily fracture from inside — perhaps the populace is too blind and ensnared for revolution to occur; but it will drive itself into disaster. Being now a product of the Jews, whose primal urge is destruction, America will destroy itself — whether through economics, foreign policy, and/or domestic policy (only wherein the populace is driven to such a dire state of un-health that it can no longer project power economically or internationally). Only from the pieces that remain after collapse — *if* any remain — will something akin to a racially homogeneous paradise again arise.

We are up against *impossibility.* Salvation will come only with utter collapse. Enablers of the Jewish system, who are potentially far worse than the Jews themselves, have complete control over nearly everything. Distraction and fear are their means. *Only a god can save us.*[20] This means the end of all. That is, god must be death.

How is it that we are born into a time of bondage, into a world flipped upside down? This "radical transvaluation of values" began with the Jews, for it was "with the Jews that the *revolt of the slaves* [began] in the sphere *of morals*; that revolt which has behind it a history of two millennia, and which at the present day has only moved out of our sight, because it — has achieved victory."[21] This Jewish victory undoubtedly explains how so many can believe the lies media, academia, churches, and governments tell, and how we can all disagree — about *everything*. It certainly seems as if all were meaningless — meaningless or a laughable simulation. Why are we in a world where people we know "vote"? Or "vote" for satanic "leaders"? One cannot vote oneself out of this really hopeless situation. Voting is a fool's game — *a vote is only consent to the tyrannical rule of the Judeo-system.*

We must yearn and fight for the end of this system. If we have the means, we must do everything we can to accelerate it. This would be doing God's work. One can read the very words of the Führer: *Christianity is a Jewish tool of enslavement.* Then one can read recent books on how the Führer "actually supported" Christianity. Why even bother with this nonsense? How can anyone even make sense of the world — this world where *right is wrong* and *good is bad*? The current order is good for one thing: ending. Wars are theater. Media is the tool of Satan. Jews are Satan's emissaries on earth. Academics are hate-filled, spiteful Marxists. Politicians are lying stooges. The military has no values beyond being a test bed for social experimentation and keeping its sights trained on the enemies of Israel.

Many good Germanic men and women died in the two world wars and in all the Jew-and-money-driven conflicts since. For what? *For our willing thralldom.* How did Germany lose the Great War? The "stab in the back"? No. So many *Germans* were *complicit defeatists.* Germany had something to fight, live, and die for — and still they lost. Europe was European then. Germany was White.

---

[20] Martin Heidegger, *Der Spiegel* interview (1966).
[21] Nietzsche, *On the Genealogy of Morals*, Essay 1, §7.

And, for what? So many Germans *still* longed for the Judeo-Marxist heel. How did Germany lose World War II? They had the world within their grasp. They lost because the Germanic people revolted against themselves, at the behest of Jews. The Germanic people chose to forfeit a promising, thriving future. Now they have a disintegrating imperium. In a few generations, they will have nothing. It will have changed to migrant hands. No Germans left. But what does it matter? The remaining Germans don't care to fight for what's theirs anyway; indeed, many want to marry up the poor migrants and make little mocha-colored babies to obliterate their leftist self-hate for all time. What did the Jews Louis Nizer, Theodore Kaufman, and Kalergi say? *Germany must perish!* What better way to end Aryans than to get them to end themselves? Ed Bernays argued that the task of the modern propagandist is to make the consumer beg for more, to create the perception that the desired end comes to the consumer of his own volition; he would be pleased with the state of today's manufactured leftism! Added to this, the leftover Germans want to fight for Israel and America — this is to say, *fight for the Jews.* Yes, Germany lost the wars. Now the European world gets what it deserves.

Apocalyptic tales and movements carry the destruction that heralds the coming or return of God. This describes the Trimurti: creation (Brahma) is now destroyed (Shiva); if creation again follows destruction and death, then it will be preserved (Vishnu) until the next downfall. In this Kali-Yuga, there is largely nothing worth preserving. The time of Vishnu is gone; it left us with the departure of Adolf Hitler, the ninth avatar. Kalki, Vishnu's tenth avatar, will come with Shiva. It is difficult to imagine that Brahma will flourish again, for the world is wrought with evil urges. But *God can conquer all things.*

We are the Sons and Daughters of Shiva. Our purpose is the restoration of God and Nature. In this time of evil urges — *in the time of the Demiurge* — we focus our efforts on accelerating the coming collapse. We prepare for the coming of Kalki and Shiva; what follows in their wake is beyond us.